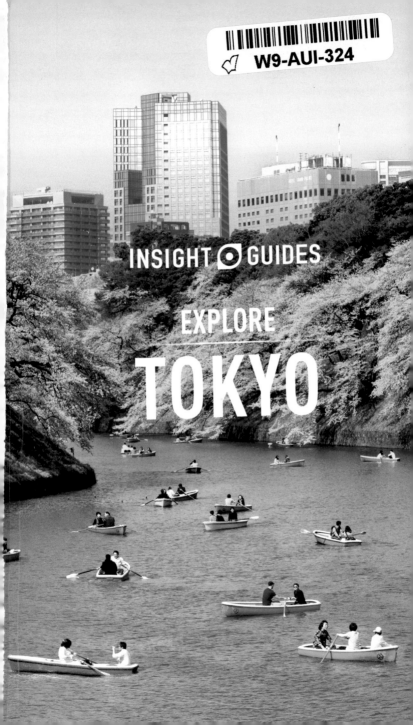

INSIGHT 💿 GUIDES

EXPLORE
TOKYO

PLAN & BOOK
YOUR TAILOR-MADE TRIP

BRAZIL **CHILE** **ECUADOR**

TAILOR-MADE TRIPS & UNIQUE EXPERIENCES CREATED BY LOCAL TRAVEL EXPERTS AT INSIGHTGUIDES.COM/HOLIDAYS

Insight Guides has been inspiring travellers with high-quality travel content for over 45 years. As well as our popular guidebooks, we now offer the opportunity to book tailor-made private trips completely personalised to your needs and interests.
By connecting with one of our local experts, you will directly benefit from their expertise and local know-how, helping you create memories that will last a lifetime.

HOW INSIGHTGUIDES.COM/HOLIDAYS WORKS

STEP 1

Pick your dream destination and submit an enquiry, or modify an existing itinerary if you prefer.

STEP 2

Fill in a short form, sharing details of your travel plans and preferences with a local expert.

STEP 3

Your local expert will create your personalised itinerary, which you can amend until you are completely satisfied.

STEP 4

Book securely online. Pack your bags and enjoy your holiday! Your local expert will be available to answer questions during your trip.

BENEFITS OF PLANNING & BOOKING AT
INSIGHTGUIDES.COM/HOLIDAYS

PLANNED BY LOCAL EXPERTS
The Insight Guides local experts are hand-picked, based on their experience in the travel industry and their impeccable standards of customer service.

SAVE TIME & MONEY
When a local expert plans your trip, you save time and money when you book, even during high season. You won't be charged for using a credit card either.

TAILOR-MADE TRIPS
Book with Insight Guides, and you will be in complete control of the planning process, from the initial selections to amending your final itinerary.

BOOK & TRAVEL STRESS-FREE
Enjoy stress-free travel when you use the Insight Guides secure online booking platform. All bookings come with a money-back guarantee.

WHAT OTHER TRAVELLERS THINK ABOUT TRIPS BOOKED
AT INSIGHTGUIDES.COM/HOLIDAYS

Trip to Portugal

Every step of the planning process and the trip itself was effortless and exceptional. Our special interests, preferences and requests were accommodated resulting in a trip that exceeded our expectations.

Corinne, USA   ★★★★★

Trip to Vietnam

The organization was superb, the drivers professional, and accommodation quite comfortable. I was well taken care of! My thanks to your colleagues who helped make my trip to Vietnam such a great experience.

Heather   ★★★★★

CONTENTS

ART ENTHUSIASTS

Bounce around Roppongi's Art Triangle (route 3), then dip into Harajuku's anarchic Design Festa gallery (route 4) or the contemporary galleries of Fukagawa (route 10).

RECOMMENDED ROUTES FOR...

CHILDREN

Youngsters will love riding the monorail and giant Ferris wheel in Odaiba (route 12) and the cable car and fantasy galleons at Hakone (route 15). For toys, there's also Kiddyland in Harajuku (route 4).

ESCAPING THE CROWDS

Meiji-jingu's grounds (route 4) can be a haven of peace, but to escape the crowds fully, head to the Kiyosumi Garden (route 10) or day trip to the hills surrounding Kamakura (route 14) or Nikko (route 16).

FOOD AND DRINK

Toyosu Fish Market, opened in 2018 (route 11), is a must, as is Isetan's fantastic food hall (route 6). Journey out to Kawagoe (tour 13) to enjoy traditional dishes in an old Edo setting.

HISTORICAL TOKYO

Circuit the Imperial Palace (route 1), learn about the city's history at the Edo-Tokyo Museum (route 10) and get a grand overview at Tokyo National Museum (route 7).

PARKS AND GARDENS

Chinzan-so (route 8) is a magnificent traditional garden. The Imperial Palace grounds and Hibiya Park (route 1) are worth seeing, as is Shinjuku National Garden (route 6). Yoyogi Park (route 4) is great for people watching.

SCIENCE AND TECHNOLOGY

Check out the Miraikan in Odaiba (route 12), Tokyo's best science museum, while in Shinjuku (route 6) there's the NTT Intercommunication Centre.

SHOPPING

Fashionistas should set their compasses for Ginza (route 2), Aoyama and Harajuku (route 4), and Shibuya (route 5). For local crafts, Asakusa (route 9) and Yanaka (route 7) have rich pickings.

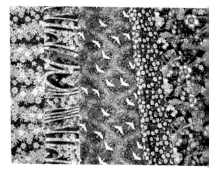

INTRODUCTION

An introduction to Tokyo's geography, customs and culture, plus illuminating background information on cuisine, history and what to do when you're there.

EXPLORE TOKYO

The world's largest megalopolis is not the most obvious place to discover on foot. However, walking through Tokyo is the best way to experience the city's fascinating history, electrifying hyperactivity and pockets of serenity.

At first glance, Tokyo comes across as a haphazard urban experiment in danger of spinning out of control. Closer examination reveals an organically evolved spoke-and-ring system with the Imperial Palace at its centre. The city's central 23 wards *(ku)* are home to 9.3 million people and interact like a huddle of micro-cities, each wired up by a complex but highly efficient system of underground and overground railway tracks.

Tokyo Prefecture (Tokyo-to) covers 2,188 sq km (845 sq miles), including 27 smaller cities, 14 towns and 27,000 islands, while the wider metropolitan area has a population exceeding 38 million. From neighbouring prefectures, millions more head into the centre every day to work and play – you will seldom escape the crowds, but that doesn't mean that you won't also be able to find havens of peace and tranquillity.

TRADITION AND CULTURE

For all its modernity, Tokyo is a city imbued with the past, where the traditions and culture of Edo (Tokyo's pre-mid-19th-century name) are cherished. Between its Postmodernist architecture and elevated expressways lie hundreds of temples, shrines and Buddhist statues. You can find the city's premier Buddhist temple in Asakusa, the top Shinto shrine Meiji-jingu in Harajuku and the controversial shrine Yasukuni-jinja near the spacious grounds of the Imperial Palace, the peaceful eye at the centre of Tokyo's storm.

Even though it lacks the greenery of other major cities, Tokyo has a number of formal gardens – often remnants of old Edo estates – where you can enjoy quiet contemplation and the passing of the seasons with beautiful flower displays. There's also a wide range of craft shops and schools for the traditional arts that help maintain skills honed over centuries. Look carefully and you will begin to see how this illustrious heritage is reflected in the designs and meticulous attention to detail of Tokyo's skyscrapers, transport system, modern-art galleries and even hi-tech electronics.

GETTING AROUND

Even though the city is spread out, getting around is easily done using the

Tokyo skyline

subway and the Japan Railways (JR) Yamanote line. The latter's egg-shaped track takes roughly an hour to complete a full loop around the inner city. Many of Tokyo's top sights, as well as major hotels and nightspots, are located at or near one of its stops. Partly shadowing the Yamanote beneath ground, but describing a wider circle that takes in areas east of the Sumida River, is the Oedo subway line.

Places outside the Yamanote line tend to form part of Shitamachi ('Low City'), such as Asakusa and Ryogoku, or represent the modern face of the city, such as the futuristic landfill island of Odaiba.

LIFE IN TOKYO

Visitors to Tokyo are likely to receive the impression of a well-fed, stylishly dressed and orderly society. Despite recent recessions and Japan's 2011 tsunami and nuclear disaster, Tokyo's standard of living remains high – to the outside eye it appears hardly reduced from the giddy days of the late 1980s – and the city is now busy gearing up for the 2020 Tokyo Olympics. Nevertheless, one segment of the population that has grown in recent years is the homeless, some vagrants, many of them elderly or victims of economic hard times. Remarkably, their 'homes' – cardboard boxes and blue tarpaulin tents in the city's major parks – are kept neat and tidy.

DIVERSITY AND COURTESY

Although Japan as a whole remains strikingly mono-cultural, Tokyo is slowly becoming an increasingly diverse and international metropolis. Young people are attracted to the city's less restricted lifestyles. Foreign students come to study, expats to fulfil contracts. Travel-

Islands of garbage

Tokyo has come up with an ingenious solution to deal with the mountains of garbage generated by its millions of citizens. Tokyo Bay is home to the euphemistically named Dream Island (Yume no Shima), which is composed entirely of rubbish. Started in the 1960s, Yume no Shima has since been covered by topsoil and now hosts a sports park, tropical greenhouse and waste facility. The building of further 'Dream Islands' in Tokyo Bay continues, although it is feared that this could end up affecting shipping lanes in the future.

In the past few decades the city's garbage-disposal rules have become increasingly stringent. Visitors can do their part by separating their rubbish into burnables (kitchen waste, cloth and paper), non-burnables (plastics, metals and ceramics) and recyclables (PET bottles, newspapers, cardboard and batteries). You will find dump-bins for each kind of waste in most public facilities, including railway and subway stations.

A sociable drink in Asakusa

lers make money (by teaching English or working in bars and clubs) and have fun. Today, the city has about 420,000 resident foreigners, with large numbers of Koreans, Chinese, Japanese-Brazilians, Filipinos and some Westerners settling here.

Few cities in the world can be so populous and yet so cordial in welcoming guests. Tokyoites might not throw their homes open to you (many live in cramped shoebox apartments), but they will often go out of their way to treat you with courtesy and be helpful, even when their English-language skills fail them. Take the trouble to learn a little Japanese before arriving and you will encounter an even warmer welcome. For some pointers on etiquette, see page 126.

CLIMATE

Apart from the regular four distinct seasons, Tokyo also has a humid rainy season, which runs from June through to September. Spring, especially late March to early April when the cherry blossoms are out, is delightful. Summers bring humid, subtropical heat well into September, when strong winds and typhoons are common. Autumn has a high sunshine count. Days are often blessed with clear, blue skies, the evenings pleasantly cool and the foliage superb. Winters are relatively mild and snow-free.

FABULOUS FESTIVALS

Matsuri (festivals) have always been integral to the life of Tokyo, and hardly a week goes by without a celebration. Timing your visit to attend one is highly recommended, since not only can they be colourful affairs but they are also a chance to see the usually decorous Japanese letting their hair and inhibitions down. Top events include May's Sanja Matsuri, August's Fukagawa Matsuri

> ## Bus and cycle tours
>
> Tired of walking? Organised half- and full-day bus tours of the city and surroundings with English guides and often hotel pick-ups can be arranged via Hato Bus (tel: 3435 6081; www.hatobus.com), Japan Gray Line (tel: 5275 6525; www.jgl.co.jp/inbound) and Sunrise Tours (tel: 75341 1413; www.jtb.co.jp).
>
> Tokyo Great Cycling Tour (tel: 4590 2995; www.tokyocycling.jp) offers seven guided cycle-tour options, ranging between two-and-a-half and six hours, from ¥5,000–10,000. Routes take in Tokyo Bay, Fukagawa and Odaiba, while the Edo Route takes you across to Ryogoku, home of sumo.
>
> For people on a budget, the city even offers free guided tours by volunteer providers in several different languages (www.gotokyo.org/en/guide-services).

Shibuya crossing from above

Asakusa rickshaws at rush hour

and October's Kawagoe Matsuri. Linked to the seasons and to religious beliefs, *matsuri* not only give thanks, petition the gods for favours and promote community solidarity; they also celebrate the sheer joy of life.

DON'T LEAVE TOKYO WITHOUT...

Eating sushi off a mini bullet train. The fish arrives in front of your table on a track that circles popular *kaitenzushi* (conveyor belt sushi) restaurant Katsu Midori in Shibuya. See page 115.

Taking a walk in Yoyogi Park. People watching doesn't get any better than at this green oasis, particularly on weekends and during the hanami cherry blossom viewing season. See page 47.

Having a night out on the town in Roppongi, Shibuya or Shinjuku. Tokyo is justifiably famous for its nightlife, which runs the gamut from the kitschy Robot Restaurant to world-class discotheques and rock clubs. See page 120.

Getting lost in youth districts Shimokitazawa or Koenji. Humming with countless funky cafes, bars, bookstores and boutiques, Shimokitazawa and Koenji offer an experience of Japanese creative culture without the crass commercialism of downtown.

Visiting Toyusu Market. Opened in late 2018, this gleaming new complex includes meat and vegetable markets, restaurants, and the world's largest fish wholesale market, moved from the iconic Tsukiji Market. See page 77.

Slurping a bowl of ramen from a greasy spoon. Ramen is now popular worldwide, but there's nothing like eating it in Tokyo, where it will cost you half as much and taste twice as good. Don't forget to slurp noisily! See page 18.

Touring the Ghibli Museum. Get lost in the world of Totaro at the Ghibli Museum, the only theme park devoted to the works of legendary animator Hayao Miyazaki. See page 25.

Ascending to the Tokyo Sky Tree. The world's third-tallest structure at 634 meters was completed in 2010 and is an engineering marvel that offers unrivalled views of the planet's largest urban sprawl. See page 42.

Spending the night in a capsule or love hotel. Capsule hotels define the bare minimum in accommodations, while love hotels are maximal expressions of sensual kitsch and excess. Take your pick! See page 100.

Getting arty. The National Art Centre, Suntory Museum of Art and Mori Art Museum form the three corners of the project Art Triangle Roppongi. Keep your ticket stub after visiting any of these three museums and it will entitle you to reduced entry at each of the others. A map showing other galleries in the area is also available at each museum or online at www.mori.art.museum/eng/atro/index.html. Tokyo Art Beat (www.tokyoartbeat.com) provides comprehensive exhibition listings in English.

Crowds on Takeshita Street in Harajuku

TOP TIPS FOR VISITING TOKYO

Opening hours. Generally you will find stores open from 10am or 11am to 7pm or 8pm, with a few places staying open even later. Sunday trading is the norm, and if shops do close it will typically be on a Monday or Wednesday.

Palace tours. The only time the general public is allowed to see the inner grounds of the Imperial Palace (Kokyo) is on 23 December (the emperor's birthday) and 2 January, when the emperor and other key members of the imperial family stand on a balcony in front of the reception building and wave to thousands of wellwishers. Avoid the crowds by signing up for a free place on one of the two official daily tours (Tue–Sat) into the palace grounds; see www.kunaicho.go.jp for details.

Visitor information. The best place for information about the city is the Tokyo Tourist Information Centre (1F Tokyo Metropolitan Government No. 1 Building, 2-8-1 Nishi-Shinjuku, Shinjuku-ku; tel: 5321-3077; www.gotokyo.org; daily 9.30am–6.30pm). Come here to find out about 10 free guided tours of the city.

Park walking tours. Free 90-minute walking tours of Ueno Park are conducted in English by volunteers on Wed, Fri, Sat and Sun at 10.30am and 1.30pm. They depart from in front of the tourist information booth next to the National Museum of Western Art on the eastern side of the park.

Smoking. This is banned in many public places, including on all public transport and in shops and public buildings. Restaurants and bars, however, do allow smoking, although many now do so in designated areas only. Smoking on the street is also being clamped down on in some of the inner-city wards, including Chuo-ku and Shinjuku-ku.

Toilets. Public toilets can be found at most train and subway stations, as well as in department stores and shopping complexes. Occasionally you will come across squat toilets, but more often than not what you will find is a high-tech toilet, where the lid rises and falls as you enter and leave.

Rail passes. If you are planning to travel extensively around Japan, buying a JR Japan Rail Pass (www.japanrailpass.net) may be useful. It's best to buy it before you arrive in Japan, although some stations within the country are trialling selling the passes at their offices until March 2020. The pass is valid for seven, 14 or 21 consecutive days. For travels closer to Tokyo, the JR East Pass (www.jreast.co.jp) is likely to be a better deal.

Bicycle rental. Intrepid travellers may want to try cycling around Tokyo. Major roads can be perilous, but if you stick to the back roads, bikes offer a great way to get intimate with the city at surface level. Tokyo by Bike (www.tokyobybike.com) has lots of helpful information about bike rentals.

Discount travel. Active sightseers can purchase a one-day economy pass (¥900) covering both metro systems, or a one-day Tokyo Combination Ticket (¥1,590) for use on all JR, metro and bus lines in the Tokyo region. Tickets are sold at pass offices at major stations.

Enoden Railway at Enoshima

There are also local festivals, especially in the summer, that often seem more like community street parties, with plenty of food and drink and spectacular historical recreations, such as the interment of the first Tokugawa shogun, held in Nikko biannually on 18 May and 17 October.

SHAKY GROUND

The 2011 9.0 megaquake 370 kilometers away from Tokyo reminded citizens of the precarious state in which they go about their lives. Japan lies above the confluence of four tectonic plates: the Eurasian, North American, Philippine and Pacific, and is home to 20 percent of the world's most powerful earthquakes. The tsunami resulting from the 2011 Great East Japan Earthquake (also called the Tohoku earthquake) took over 18,000 lives (the nuclear disaster forced thousands from their homes, but only one direct fatality from radiation exposure has so far been acknowledged). Closer to home, the Great Kanto Earthquake of 1923 flattened large parts of Tokyo and claimed over 58,000 lives, while continuing aftershocks from the 2011 event, and several smaller quakes since, provide regular reminders of the city's vulnerability to a major tremor.

Even with improved building regulations and techniques, it is estimated by the Japanese government that a quake measuring 7.3 on the Richter scale hitting the city at evening rush hour would kill 13,000 inhabitants and cause $US1 trillion worth of damage. For tips on what to do in the event of a tremor, see page 125.

ESCAPING THE CITY

For all its human energy and consumer glitz, there comes a time when even the most hardened urbanites wish to shake off Tokyo's concrete shell. Thanks to an efficient rail system, escape is easily at hand. Depending what you fancy, choose from old-world Kawagoe, Zen-like Kamakura, the beautiful lakeside national parkland of Hakone or temple-crammed Nikko. All of these – not to mention broad Pacific beaches and the soaring peak of Mount Fuji – are within two hours' reach of downtown.

It should be remembered, however, that fully leaving the city behind can be a challenging prospect – especially at the weekend, when it seems as if all of Tokyo is also heading for the great outdoors.

NATIONAL HOLIDAYS

Three times a year almost all of Japan is on holiday. Avoid trips during the New Year (roughly 25 Dec–4 Jan), Golden Week (29 Apr–5 May) and Obon (7–10 days centring on 15 Aug).

In a Shimbashi izakaya.

FOOD & DRINK

Tokyo is justly renowned as one of the culinary capitals of the world, and the variety and quality of its food and drink are unrivalled. Here you will sample the very best, from sake and exquisite kaiseki ryori morsels to delicious coffee and croissants.

Japanese cuisine is a sensation for the eyes and the taste buds. Seasoning is minimal, and every chef takes freshness very seriously. Tokyo claims many Japanese dishes as its own, but its cuisine also reflects that of the entire country. The city's gastronomic offerings also encompass other Asian cuisines, as well as those of Europe, Africa and the Americas.

WHERE TO EAT

Neighbourhood Japanese diners are not usually fancy, but the prices are low. Noodle shops are found everywhere, ranging from venerable establishments to cheap stand-and-slurp counters. Conveyor-belt sushi is good value, while *okonomiyaki* (a kind of savoury pancake containing a choice of ingredients) make for fun dining. Department stores and shopping malls always offer a wide range of restaurants, usually located on a single floor.

In the evening, *izakaya* (restaurant-pubs) serve reasonably priced local food and alcohol. They typically identify themselves with a string of red lanterns hanging over the door. *Izakaya* do not serve full-course meals, and there is no pressure to eat quickly. Order beer, sake or *shochu* (a vodka-like spirit) and sample a few dishes such as *sashimi*, grilled fish, *yakitori* or tofu. End your meal with rice or noodles.

If you are at a loss for what to eat, the lavish food halls in department store basements known as *depachika* can satisfy any taste. The best can be found in smart department stores like Isetan and Mitsukoshi.

What will it cost?

Eating out in Tokyo is not as expensive as one might expect, especially the lunch set menus for under ¥1,500. For dinner expect to pay about ¥3,000–5,000 per head. Top places can go up to ¥10,000 per person or more.

JAPANESE CUISINE

Japanese cooking focuses on accentuating the inherent flavours rather than enhancing them with sauces. Meals are based on fish, vegetables, seaweed and tofu. Eggs, meat and poultry are used in limited quantities, while

Fresh sashimi

dairy foods play barely any part in the traditional diet. Portions are small and served in bite-sized morsels, with ingredients reflecting the seasons. Presentation is equally important, as the Japanese believe you also eat with your eyes. Plates, bowls and utensils are made of ceramic, glass, stone, wood or lacquer. Like the ingredients, they are changed to fit the season and to match the food they are showcasing.

Sushi and sashimi

The Japanese love to eat seafood as close as possible to its natural state – either as sashimi, slices of raw fish served with a dip of soy sauce and wasabi (Japanese horseradish), or as sushi, on vinegared rice. The best-known sushi is the Tokyo style known as *nigiri-sushi*. Some of the best *sushiya* (sushi shops) are found near the former fish market in Tsukiji.

Although guaranteed to be memorable, dining at a top sushi restaurant can be a dauntingly expensive experience. The cheaper alternative is a *kaiten-zushi* shop, where small dishes of sushi pass by on a conveyor belt, sometimes for as little as ¥100 per plate.

The concept of eating small patties of vinegared rice topped with cuts of raw seafood originated in the days of Edo and is still called Edomae sushi, because the seafood was caught in the bay in front of the city.

Hotpots

One of the pleasures of visiting Japan in winter is the chance to sample a variety of hearty hotpots. Known as *nabe-ryori* (casserole cuisine), every area has its own distinctive variations. Styles range from Hokkaido's salmon-based *ishikari-nabe* to Tokyo's *yanagawa-nabe*, which is made with *dojo* (an eel-like loach).

A favourite among locals – and something of an acquired taste for visitors – is *oden*. Made with *daikon* radish, potatoes, whole hard-boiled eggs, tofu, fish-paste patties and other ingredients, this hotpot, served with a dab of mustard, is one of the standard dishes served at *yatai* street stalls and convenience stores.

Grilled food

Since Edo times, *unagi*, grilled eel served on a bed of rice, has had a reputation for giving energy during the summer, but it's just as delicious at other times of the year. Another grilled food is *yakitori*, skewers of chicken, often cooked over charcoal. Almost every part of the bird is eaten, from the breast to the heart. Gourmet versions can be had in upscale restaurants, but most people prefer the smoky street stalls.

Noodles

Noodles are the original Japanese fast food. *Soba* noodles are made with buckwheat flour – the best being *te-uchi*, freshly prepared and chopped by hand.

SHOPPING

Tokyo is one of the world's premier shopping destinations. The options are immense, from centuries-old emporiums selling traditional crafts and prestigious department stores to cheerful novelty shops where everything is ¥100.

In a city where a good deal of status is attached to brand names, being seen with the right designer-label bag defines the shopper. Even if you don't know the brand, you can pretty much be assured of quality, a principle of Japanese manufacturing applied to everything from integrated circuits to the glaze on an earthenware pot. The Japanese take great pride in their work, a legacy of the old craft and trade guilds and the country's artisan traditions.

In Japan 'the customer is always right' becomes 'the customer is God'. Service here is an art; the wrapping, decorating and packaging of goods is all done with remarkable speed and dexterity, and staff will invariably be super-polite.

DEPARTMENT STORES AND MALLS

Department stores such as Isetan, Mitsukoshi and Takashimaya are regarded as institutions and like to think of themselves more as cultural centres than just marketplaces. You can find almost any product in these full-service stores and, if the weather is fine, you may be able to relax in the rooftop playground, beer garden or golf range, while more sophisticated pleasures are provided by in-house art galleries. At the other extreme, Don Quijote has become a powerhouse by pioneering the discount department store for Japan's deflation era.

As a note, the morning ritual (usually at 10am) when a department store opens its doors is well worth attending. Uniformed staff, immaculately turned out, stand at the main entrance and at the top of the escalators, bowing to each customer in turn.

One big change to Tokyo's shopping and leisure scene has been the emergence of state-of-the-art living complexes where visitors can be provided with everything they need for an entire day. Developments such as Roppongi Hills and Tokyo Midtown in Roppongi, with their striking architecture and cultural facilities, have become destinations in their own right quite apart from the shopping opportunities they provide.

Even smaller malls such as the chic Ando Tadao-designed Omotesando

Hills and Venus Fort in Odaiba are worth checking out, the latter having an artificial sky that cycles through dawn-to-dusk lighting effects.

ELECTRONICS

For electronics and hi-tech devices Akihabara, a couple of stops south of Ueno on the Yamanote line, offers many competitively priced stores such as Laox, which stocks duty-free overseas models, and Yodobashi Camera. You can also pick up good deals at Bic Camera, with its main store in Yurakucho opposite the Tokyo International Forum and other branches in Ikebukuro, Shinjuku and Shibuya.

FASHION

For high-end fashion and designer labels, head to Marunouchi and Ginza, where you will also find flagship home branches of worldwide retail successes such as Uniqlo (www.uniqlo.com) and Muji (www.muji.net).

Japanese designers rule in Aoyama and the eclectic youth-orientated stores of Harajuku, as well as in nearby Shibuya. Also well worth a browse are the trendy boutiques of Daikanyama and Naka-Meguro, both a train or subway stop away from Shibuya and Ebisu respectively.

Another dressing-up option is the so-called 'Fashion Building'. Tokyo has hundreds of these multi-floored malls that rent space to different boutiques to showcase their latest collections; they include places like La Foret (www. laforet.ne.jp) in Harajuku and Shibuya 109 (www.shibuya109.jp).

TRADITIONAL CRAFTS

If you are in the market for traditional crafts, then head to Asakusa. While here you can also explore the wide range of kitchen and tableware available in nearby Kappabashi. Rounding out this northeastern Tokyo retail experience is Ueno, where the Ameya Yokocho market area is good for cheap food, cosmetics, clothing and toys. Also good for craft souvenirs are Oriental Bazaar in Harajuku and Ito-ya in Ginza.

SHOPPING RULES

Although there are some exceptions, prices in Tokyo are generally fixed and non-negotiable. Shops accepting overseas credit cards remain relatively rare, although you shouldn't have a problem in the main department stores. Large department stores and increasing numbers of retailers targeting the tourism boom are usually happy to refund the 8 percent consumption tax to foreign customers who purchase goods over ¥5,000, but you will have to produce your passport. Many shops now have tax-free counters to make the process easier.

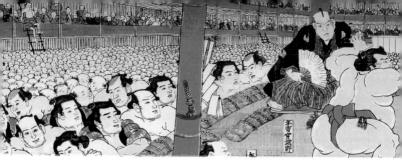

SPORTS & ENTERTAINMENT

Baseball and football get Tokyo sports fans most excited, but you can also watch sumo and martial arts in the capital. Similarly, when it comes to performing arts, the city provides an eclectic mix of the traditional and the contemporary.

With Japan gearing up to host the 2020 Olympic and Paralympic Games – which will be held in Tokyo from 24 July to 9 August and from 25 August to 6 September respectively – it hopes to attract an ever-growing number of sports fans. Several of the 1964 Summer Olympics venues will be reused for the 2020 Games, 11 new ones are to be built, and the Ryogoku Kokugikan will receive a total revamp. The location of most sites is planned within 8km (5 miles) of the Olympic Village in Tokyo Bay.

SPORTS

Sumo

Steeped in Shinto rituals, the national sport of sumo has been around for at least 2,000 years. Allegations of match-fixing and bad behaviour by wrestlers have tainted the sport in recent years, but it still commands a strong following, and witnessing a tournament may well be a highlight of your trip to Japan.

Matches between wrestlers (called *rikishi*), who can weigh up to and over 168kg (370lbs), were traditionally held at shrines such as Yasukuni-jinja where they still occasionally take place. They are punctuated by ritual stomping to drive evil spirits from the ring, and salt-throwing for purification.

The apprenticeship of a *rikishi* is long and harsh. Only when the wrestler makes it to the higher ranks of *ozeki* or rarely achieved *yokozuna* (grand champion) does life become easier. Those in the lower ranks become servants of the *ozeki* or *yokozuna*, running errands and scrubbing backs.

Three of sumo's six annual 15-day tournaments occur at Tokyo's Ryogoku Kokugikan sumo stadium in January, May and September. In downtimes you can visit sumo stables to observe wrestlers' morning practice sessions.

Baseball

Some of Japan's top *yakkyu* (baseball) stars have moved to the US Major Leagues, but a game at either the Tokyo Dome (near Korakuen Station; www. tokyo-dome.co.jp), home ground of the Yomuri Giants, or Meiji Jingu Stadium (near Gaienmae Station), base for the Yakult Swallows, demonstrates how the Japanese have made the sport their own.

Japan's 'second national sport' (but top spectator sport) maintains its appeal

Kokugikan Sumo Stadium mural

among the older generation. Younger Japanese seem less keen, although the Major League success of players such as Ichiro Suzuki, Masahiro Tanaka (who currently plays for the New York Yankees) and others is changing that. The season runs from April to October, culminating in the best-of-seven Japan Series between the pennant winners of the two leagues.

Football

Holding the 2002 World Cup, and winning the championship at the 2011 Women's World Cup, gave a major boost to the popularity of football (soccer) in Japan. The J-League (www.jleague.jp) football season runs from February to October, with a special Emperor's Cup event in December. The capital's two top teams, FC Tokyo and Tokyo Verdy, play at the Ajinomoto Stadium in Chofu City, western Tokyo.

THEATRE AND DANCE

Tokyo offers an interesting range of performing arts. From Japanese antiquity there is the entrancing masked stillness of *noh*, the masterful puppetry of *bunraku* and the garish stylisation of *kabuki*. Or there are outstanding performance halls for top-notch Western-style musicals, ballet and contemporary dance. Then there is avant-garde *butoh* or experimental theatre at one of Tokyo's tiny black-box venues.

Bunraku

The adult puppet theatre of *bunraku* is an art dating back to the 7th century, when itinerant Chinese and Korean performers presented semi-religious puppet plays. As with *kabuki* and *noh*, the plays deal with themes such as revenge and sacrifice, love and rejection, reincarnation and futility.

Each major puppet is manipulated by three operators, a logistic marvel in itself. In theory, the audience does not notice all the shuffling of the black-clad professional puppeteers, concentrating instead on the puppets, which are roughly one-third of the size of a human. The real tour de force, though, are the narrators – the *gidayu* performers – who speak, gesture and weep from a kneeling position at stage left.

Kabuki

In Japanese *kabuki* translates as 'song-dance skill', with no mention of theatre, although the performances themselves are highly stylised and theatrical. In the early 16th century the word *kabuki* meant 'avant-garde' and referred to all-female performances, often of a licentious nature. The Tokugawa shogunate banned female performers in 1629. This started the all-male tradition that continues today; actresses are only allowed for certain special events.

The main *kabuki* theatres are the newly renovated Kabuki-za, the Shimbashi Embujo (6-12-2 Ginza, Chuo-ku; tel: 3541 2600; station: Shimbashi) and the National Theatre. Most programmes span three or four hours, with generous intervals for tea drinking and socialising;

A poster advertising a kabuki performance

for most visitors a single act or around an hour or so will be sufficient to get a taste.

Noh

This minimalist theatre is a development from early temple plays. Aristocratic patronage demanded esoteric poetry, sophisticated language and a refined simplicity of movement, precisely what you see six centuries later. It is difficult to describe *noh* – words like 'ethereal', 'inaccessible' and 'subtle' spring to mind. Fortunately, some English translations are available. Catch noh performances at the National Noh Theatre (4-18-1 Sendagaya, Shibuya-ku; tel: 3423 1331; www.ntj.jac.go.jp; station: Sendagaya).

Western-style theatre

Translations of foreign plays and musicals, imported from London and New York, are very popular and range from Chekhov to *Cats*. Most are performed in Japanese by Japanese dancers and singers. Performances can be a mixed experience.

For a very Japanese take on musical theatre, attend a performance by the Takarazuka Revue (http://kageki.hankyu.co.jp), an all-female song-and-dance extravaganza. It is unashamedly flamboyant and romantic, with gorgeous costumes. Watched mainly by middle-aged housewives and young women, the shows are held at the Takarazuka Grand Theater across the river from the Takarazuka Hotel.

Tokyo also offers a lively experimental theatre scene, known as the *shogekijo*

('little theatre') movement. Much of the activity centres on the counterculture district of Shimokitazawa, west of Shibuya, where there are many small venues.

Classical music and ballet

A dedicated following exists for classical music and ballet, with performances by domestic companies at venues such as Tokyo Opera City and the New National Theatre on the western side of Shinjuku, and Bunkamura's Orchard Hall in Shibuya.

Keep an eye out for performances by the celebrated Tokyo-based Asami Maki Ballet (www.ambt.jp) and the K-Ballet Company (www.k-ballet.co.jp); the latter is headed up by Tetsuya Kumakawa, who has also performed with the UK's Royal Ballet.

Contemporary dance

Tokyo has a fervent audience for boldly experimental dance performances, which can involve innovative multimedia. Performances are held at Session House (158 Yaraicho, Shinjuku-ku; tel: 3266 0461; www.session-house.net; station: Kagurazaka), Karas Apparatus (5-11-15, Ogikubo; tel: 6276 9136; www.st-karas.com; station: Ogikubo), Setagaya Public Theatre (http://setagaya-pt.jp/en) and the New National Theatre, Tokyo (http://www.nntt.jac.go.jp/english).

Butoh

Originally called a 'dance of darkness', *butoh* strives not for beauty and physi-

お帰りなさいませ！ご主人様・お嬢様！

A distinctive Akihabara Maids Café sign

cal grace, but to depict the inhumanity and discord of existence, with cathartic results for the audience. This internationally renowned avant-garde dance form is becoming more widely accepted in its home country. *Butoh* performances take place at the Setagaya Public Theatre, Session House and numerous smaller halls. Two of the best-known companies are Dairakudakan (www.dairakudakan.com) and Sankaijuku (www.sankaijuku.com).

POPULAR MUSIC

Japanese devotion to music is legendary, and as the capital of the world's second-biggest music market, Tokyo is at the centre of it. From its vast stadiums to its smoky dives, from ancient sounds to the cutting edge, Tokyo boasts a lifetime's worth of musical experience any night of the week; for suggestions of venues to check out, see page . With an increasing number of bands touring Tokyo and more foreign musicians choosing to make it their home, its music scene is becoming progressively more international. CD and vinyl buffs can also indulge in the world's most diverse market for record shopping.

Martial arts

Judo, karate, aikido, *kyudo* (archery) and *kendo* (fencing) all have regular championships or demonstration events, which are usually held at the Nippon Budokan.

Listings

You can pick up a free copy of the monthly listings magazine *Metropolis* (http://metropolisjapan.com) each Friday at major hotels, restaurants, bars and shops where foreigners gather.

Otaku culture

Otaku – originally a derogatory term for people with pathologically obsessive interests in *anime* (Japanese animation) and *manga* (Japanese comics) – has now become synonymous with Japanese cool as well as an economy worth billions of dollars.

As well as being home to hundreds of electronics and software shops, Akihabara (*Akiba* to the faithful) is the first place many fans head to find maid cafés (where waitresses dress up in costumes), *cosplay* hobby outlets (for dressing up as a favourite *anime* character) and the like. The Tokyo Anime Center (www.animecenter.jp), in Shinjuku, is a showroom for the newest and best-known *anime*, with a screening room, exhibition galleries, shop and studio where visitors can listen to actors recording dialogue.

In Tokyo's western suburbs is the Ghibli Museum (www.ghibli-museum.jp), celebrating the animated movies of Studio Ghibli, such as Hayao Miyazaki's *Spirited Away*. The store Mandarake (www.mandarake.co.jp) is a temple for manga and anime fanatics, with branches in Nakano and Shibuya.

17th century woodblock print of the Nihombashi Bridge

HISTORY: KEY DATES

Tokyo's rise from humble fishing village to contemporary, economic powerhouse stretches back over a millennium, during which time it has survived practically the worst that nature and mankind could throw at it.

PRE-EDO PERIODS

628AD   Senso-ji (Asakusa Kannon) is founded after two brothers discover a golden statue of the bodhisattva Kannon in their fishing nets.

1180   The first recorded use of the name Edo (meaning 'Rivergate') for the area later to become Tokyo.

1457   Ota Dokan, the poet and monk celebrated as Tokyo's founder, builds a castle at Edo. First land reclamation project.

1590   Tokugawa Ieyasu begins construction of a new fortress on site of Ota Dokan's old castle.

EDO PERIOD (1603–1868)

1603   The beginning of the 265-year rule of the Tokugawa dynasty, governing from their military base at Edo.

1657   The Furisode (Long Sleeves) Fire destroys most of the city and kills a quarter of Edo's inhabitants.

1707   Ash covers Edo after an eruption of Mount Fuji.

1742   Roughly 4,000 die in Edo after a series of floods and storms.

1780   The city's population reaches 1.3 million. Edo is probably the largest city in the world at this time.

1853   Commodore Matthew Perry's Black Ships appear in Tokyo Bay, the end of Japan's 250-year isolation from the outside world.

1855   A major earthquake hits Edo, killing over 7,000 residents and destroying much of the Shitamachi area.

MEIJI PERIOD (1868–1912)

1868   Edo is renamed Tokyo.

1869   The emperor Meiji moves to Tokyo, which becomes the new capital and seat of government.

1872   Japan's first railway begins service from Yokohama to Shimbashi.

1890   The first sitting of the Imperial Diet (legislative assembly).

Some of the destruction wrought by the Great Kanto Earthquake

TAISHO AND SHOWA PERIODS (1912–89)

1920 Meiji-jingu is constructed.

1923 The Great Kanto Earthquake leaves over 100,000 people dead, and a quarter of the city is wiped out in the fire of the aftermath.

1927 A subway, the first in Asia, opens between Asakusa and Ueno.

1932 Tokyo's city limits are expanded to its current 23 wards.

1945 American B-29s firebomb the city. Over half the city is destroyed and 100,000 civilians die.

1945–52 American occupation years. General McArthur sets up headquarters in Tokyo. Post-war national reconstruction begins.

1955 The Liberal Democratic Party is formed and wins the general election. It has been the ruling party of Japan ever since.

1964 The city hosts the Olympics.

HEISEI PERIOD (1989–2019)

1989 The death of Emperor Hirohito at the Imperial Palace ushers in the new emperor Akihito and the Heisei era.

1990 The bubble economy bursts, triggering Tokyo land price slump.

1995 Members of the Aum Shinrikyo cult release sarin gas in a commuter train, killing 12 and injuring thousands.

1999 Ishihara Shintaro, an outspoken nationalist, is elected as Tokyo governor.

2002 The Fifa World Cup final is played in Tokyo following Japan and Korea's co-hosting of football tournament.

2007 Ishihara is re-elected for a third consecutive term.

2011 The 2011 9.0 earthquake, tsunami and nuclear disaster shakes Tokyo and leaves thousands dead in northeast Japan.

2012 Tokyo Skytree, the world's second tallest structure at 634 meters, opens to the public.

2013 Tokyo selected to host the 2020 summer Olympics.

2015 Thousands protest Prime Minister Abe's secrecy and security legislation in front of Parliament.

2016 Yuriko Koike is elected as the first female governor of Tokyo.

2017 Shinzo Abe wins a snap general election and begins his fourth term as Prime Minister.

2019 Citing age and ill health, Emperor Akihito abdicates on 30 April – the first Japanese emperor to do so in over 200 years. Crown Prince Naruhito is set to succeed him and reign over the Reiwa era.

BEST ROUTES

Imperial Palace

THE IMPERIAL PALACE & AROUND

After a visit to Tokyo's most controversial shrine, stroll through the peaceful Imperial Palace grounds, taking in a couple of interesting art museums and finishing up at the city's first European-style park.

DISTANCE: 5km (3 miles)
TIME: A half day
START: Kudanshita Station
END: Hibiya Station
POINTS TO NOTE: The Imperial Palace East Garden is closed on Mondays and Fridays. Volunteers offer a free two-hour walking tour around the Imperial Palace grounds on Saturdays at 1pm (meet at the gate of the Central Marunouchi entrance in Tokyo Station; www.tfwt.jp).

At the heart of the buzzing metropolis, the Imperial Palace, home to the world's oldest monarchy, stands amid the grounds of the once formidable Edo Castle. Tokyo's rise began here in 1590, when the first shogun, Tokugawa Ieyasu, chose the site as his new headquarters. When the castle was completed in 1640, it was the largest in the world.

YASUKUNI-JINJA

From Kudanshita Station, walk uphill towards the huge steel torii gate mark-ing the entrance to **Yasukuni-jinja** ❶ (www.yasukuni.or.jp). Built to enshrine the souls of around 2.5 million war dead, this controversial Shinto shrine was completed in 1869. To the rear, there is a pretty ornamental garden with a teahouse and an adjacent sumo ring where bouts are held during the shrine's spring festival.

Yushukan
Yasukuni's fascinating museum, **Yush-ukan** ❷ (daily 9am–4.30pm), houses samurai costumes, faded photos, let-ters from the front and other reminders of Japan's tragic military past, all pre-sented with a revisionist view of Japan's 20th century war making. Look out for the *kaiten*, a human suicide torpedo.

KITANOMARU PARK

Cross busy Yasukuni-dori to reach **Tayasu-mon** ❸, the entrance gate to **Kitanomaru Park** (Kitanomaru-koen). The former home of the Imperial Guard is now a wooded area with nature trails and some interesting museums.

Flowers in the East Garden   *Yasukuni jinja*

Walk south and the outline of the martial arts hall **Nippon Budokan** ❹ (www.nipponbudokan.or.jp), built for the 1964 Olympics, will come into view. The design of this striking octagonal hall, with a curving roof and what looks like a golden topknot, is based on that of the Horyu-ji Buddhist temple's Hall of Dreams near the ancient city of Nara (southwest of Tokyo). Concerts,

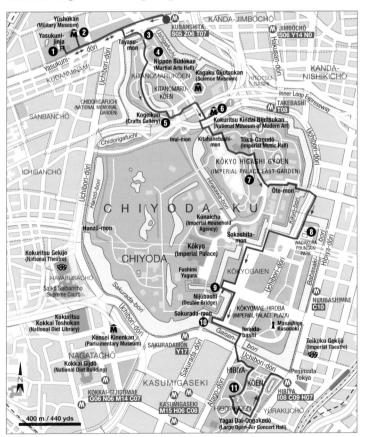

Pine trees by one of the palace moats

exhibitions and tournaments of karate, archery, judo and Japanese fencing are held here.

Continue through the park, heading to the right to reach the rewarding **Crafts Gallery ❺** (Kogeikan; www.momat. go.jp/cg; Tue–Sun 10am–5pm), which is housed in a handsome Gothic Revival-style red-brick building, erected in 1910 to accommodate the old Imperial Palace Guard. Many of the exhibits, notably ceramic items, textiles and lacquerware, are the work of craftsmen honoured as 'Living National Treasures'.

The Crafts Gallery is an annexe of the nearby **National Museum of Modern Art ❻** (Kokuritsu Kindai Bijutsukan; www.momat.go.jp; Tue–Thu, Sun 10am–5pm, Fri–Sat 10am–8pm). Besides an impressive display of paintings and sculptures by Japanese artists from the Meiji era to the present, the museum also has a few works by foreign artists such as Picasso. **L'Art et**

Mikuni, see ❶, is the museum's stylish restaurant and café.

AROUND THE IMPERIAL PALACE EAST GARDEN

Passing over the highway and a section of the old castle moat, walk through the Kitahanebashi-mon gate to enter the **Imperial Palace East Garden ❼** (Kokyo Higashi Gyoen; Tue–Thu, Sat–Sun 9am–4pm). This ornamental garden, with its inner circle of moats, was the site of Edo's original five-tiered keep. The keep burnt down in a major fire that swept Edo in 1657. The heat was apparently so intense that it melted all the gold reserves kept in the keep's vault. Only its sturdy stone base survives, but it is worth climbing this to get a view of the surroundings, including the mosaic-decorated **Imperial Music Hall** (Toka-Gagudo).

The walls of the inner moat have fared better. Huge blocks were cut from great slabs of stone brought by ship from Izu, 80km (50 miles) away.

Wadakura Fountain Park

Leave the garden through Ote Gate (Otemon), an impressive replica of the original main gate, and step into the precincts of the Outer Garden, now known as the **Imperial Palace Plaza** (Kokyomae Hiroba). The former gardens, planted with some 2,000 Japanese black pine trees and lawns in 1899, are split by wide Uchibori-dori. In the plaza's northeastern corner is the **Wadakura Foun-**

Japan's war dead

Before an important battle, soldiers sometimes exchanged the words, 'Let us meet at Yasukuni', meaning the place where their spirits would be honoured. In 1979 several Class-A war criminals were enshrined here, outraging Japan's neighbours. Every 15 August – the anniversary of the country's defeat in World War II – the controversy erupts afresh, when a ceremony is held at Yasukuni.

Kusunoki Masashing statue

The red-brick Crafts Gallery

tain Park **❽**, built to celebrate the royal wedding of the emperor and empress in 1961, and refurbished on the occasion of their son's marriage in 1995.

Continue south across the plaza to have your photograph taken against the picturesque backdrop of **Nijubashi ❾**, the Double Layer Bridge, with the graceful outline of the Fushimi Turret (Fushimi Yagura), and perhaps a swan or two gliding under the willow trees of the outer moat.

Follow the moat south to find **Sakurada-mon ❿**, dating from 1620, the largest of the remaining gates of Edo Castle. Although damaged by the Great Kanto Earthquake of 1923, the gate was rebuilt and is designated an 'Important Cultural Asset'.

HIBIYA PARK

Exit the Imperial Palace Plaza at the Iwaida Bridge (Iwaida-bashi) over the Gaisen Moat (Gaisen-bori). Cross the highway and enter **Hibiya Park ⓫** (Hibiya-koen) on your left. This 16ha (41-acre) former parade ground was restyled as Japan's first Western-style park in 1903. It remains a curious mixture of Meiji-period Japanese and European landscaping, with an original wisteria trellis, crane fountain and a Japanese garden. Among the several places to eat here, the most pleasant is **Matsumotoro**, see **❷**.

There are hundreds of cherry trees in Yasukuni's grounds, making this a prime spot for *hanami* (cherry-blossom viewing) in spring. Festivals to entertain the spirits of the dead are also held in the shrine grounds at the end of April and mid-October.

The Imperial Palace Plaza has witnessed some momentous scenes in recent history. Survivors of the Great Kanto Earthquake gathered here in 1923, and in August 1945 several members of Japan's officer corps committed *seppuku* (ritual suicide) here, in order, it is said, to atone for their failure in World War II. In the 1950s and '60s student radicals and workers rallied at the plaza to take part in sometimes violent demonstrations.

Food and drink

❶ L'ART ET MIKUNI

National Museum of Modern Art, 3-1 Kitanomaru-koen, Chiyoda-ku; tel: 3213 0392; http://lart-et-mikuni.jp; Tue–Sun 11.30am–3pm, 5.30–9pm, closed for dinner Sun; station: Takebashi; ¥¥
A giant sculpture by Japanese-American artist Isamu Noguchi stands outside this pleasant contemporary restaurant with an outdoor terrace. Chef Kiyomi Mikuni creates artistic dishes under the concept of 'fusion of French and Italian styles'.

❷ MATSUMOTORO

1-2 Hibiya-koen, Chiyoda-ku; tel: 3503 1451; www.matsumotoro.co.jp; daily 11am–2.30pm, 5–9pm; station: Hibiya; ¥¥
In the centre of Hibiya Park, try Japanese takes on Western dishes (a style known as *yoshoku*) or relax over afternoon tea.

Shoppers in Ginza

MARUNOUCHI & GINZA

There's more to the revitalised business and shopping districts of Marunouchi and Ginza than retail therapy, as you will discover on this walk along the grid-like streets to the east of the Imperial Palace.

> **DISTANCE:** 5km (3 miles)
> **TIME:** A half day
> **START/END:** Hibiya Station
> **POINTS TO NOTE:** This route follows on from the Imperial Palace walk (see page 30). It is good to start in the late afternoon, so you can see Ginza lit up at night.

Both Marunouchi and Ginza are synonymous with expensive chic; against strong competition from other quarters they retain their charm, especially for the well-heeled, middle-aged shopper. The boutiques lining Marunouchi's Naka-dori or Ginza's Chuo-dori are a roll call of designer labels. But there are also cultural treasures here, plus prime examples of heritage and contemporary architecture.

MARUNOUCHI

It's a long time since Marunouchi lived up to its name – 'within the castle walls'. The opening of Tokyo Station in 1914 put it on the modern map, and today it is enjoying a renaissance as the landowner Mitsubishi redevelops the area.

Once an anonymous street of office buildings, **Naka-dori** ❶ has blossomed into a sophisticated shopping strip. Start exploring it from the rear entrance of the **Peninsula Tokyo**, taking a moment to look up to your left just after you pass the first cross-street; poised at the hotel's corner is a gargoyle.

Idemitsu Museum of Art

Head up Naka-dori one more block and turn left to reach the **Idemitsu Museum of Art** ❷ (Idemitsu Bijutsukan; www.idemitsu.or.jp/museum; Tue–Thu, Sat–Sun 10am–5pm, Fri 10am–7pm), hidden away on the ninth floor of the same building as the Imperial Theatre. This is one of Tokyo's best private museums, housing a superb collection of Japanese ceramics, *ukiyo*-e woodblock prints, folding screens, exquisite Momoyama and early Edo-period gold-leaf genre paintings, and the 15th-century monochrome paintings of the Zen monk Sesshu. Its lounge provides a panoramic view of the Imperial Palace.

Inside Tokyo International Forum

Tokyo International Forum

Return to and cross Naka-dori, and continue for one more block, passing **Pâtisserie Sadaharu AOKI**, see ❶, to reach the striking **Tokyo International Forum** ❸ (www.t-i-forum.co.jp). Opened in 1997, the exhibition hall and theatre complex is the work of New York-based designer Rafael Vinoly. To get a bird's-eye view, go up to the seventh floor, where skywalks criss-cross the middle of a curving 60m (190ft) high glass atrium shaped like a ship's hull.

Mitsubishi Ichigokan Museum

Return to Naka-dori to find the **Mitsubishi Ichigokan Museum** ❹ (2-6-2 Marunouchi, Chiyoda-ku; http://mimt.jp; Tue–Sun 10am–8pm, Fri until 9pm). This art museum owned by industrial giant Mitsubishi focuses on works from the mid-18th to 20th centuries. It is housed

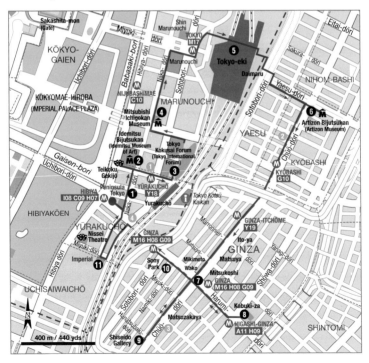

Ginza chic

in a meticulous replica of the handsome 1894 red-brick office building – the first in the area – designed by Josiah Conder.

Continue to the intersection of Naka-dori and broad Miyuki-dori, flanked by the high-rise Marunouchi and Shin-Marunouchi buildings. Turn right to face the handsome brick façade of **Tokyo Station ⑤**. This grand example of Taisho-era Western architecture, designed by Tatsuno Kingo, a former student of Conder, recently underwent a major renovation that restored the building's original lustre.

ARTIZON MUSEUM

Negotiate the pedestrian corridor beneath the station's tracks that leads from the Marunouchi to the Yaesu side of the building, emerging beside Daimaru department store facing Yaesu-dori. Walk two blocks east to the intersection with Chuo-dori and the **Artizon Museum ⑥** (Artizon Bijutsukan; 1-10-1 Kyobashi, Chuo-ku; www.bridgestone-museum.gr.jp; Tue–Sat 10am–8pm, Sun and hols 10am–6pm). The former Bridgestone Museum of Art closed in 2015 for extensive renovations, which are due to conclude in January 2020 with its reopning as the Artizon Museum. The new space will include galleries of traditional Japanese art from the Meiji period, 19th-century French Impressionist works, post-WWII abstract paintings and contemporary art.

Continue south down Chuo-dori towards Kyobashi subway station; on the way you can grab an energy boost from **GGCo. Café & Bakery**, see ❷, before tackling the next boutique-and-department-store-studded stretch of the street.

GINZA

Two of the area's best-known retail landmarks stand on the corner of the **Ginza 4-chome crossing ⑦**. The exclusive department store **Wako**, owned by the watch company Seiko, is housed in one of the few buildings to have survived the World War II air raids that flattened Ginza; it dates back to 1932. Across the road is **Mitsukoshi**, a top city department store. Also close by are **Mikimoto**, selling cultured pearls, and **Ito-ya**, a superb paper and stationery store.

Kabuki-za

From Ginza 4-chome head southeast along Harumi-dori for several blocks to reach the opulent exterior of **Kabuki-za ❽** (4-12-15 Ginza, Chuo-ku; www.kabukiweb.net). Here colourful and highly stylised *kabuki* dramas, combining music, dance and singing, are staged twice a day (usually starting at 11am and 4.30pm) during the first three weeks of the month – catching at least one act is recommended. It was founded in 1889 and rebuilt in 1924 and then again, controversially, in 2013 with a huge new tower by Kengo Kuma.

Shiseido Gallery

Ginza is also well known for its many small art galleries. A good one to head to is the **Shiseido Gallery ❾** (8-8-3 Ginza, Chuo-ku;

Lion Beer Hall

Tokyo Station

www.shiseidogroup.com/gallery; Tue–Sat 11am–7pm, Sun and hols 11am–6pm) in the basement of Shiseido Parlour, a cosmetics boutique. It features experimental art by Japanese and foreign artists. On the way there or back along Chuo-dori you will pass the **Lion Beer Hall**, see ❸.

Return to Ginza 4-chome and turn left, heading along Harumi-dori past more luxury boutiques to the **Sony Park** ❿ (www.ginzasonypark.jp; daily 5am–12.30am), an area of greenery and paths (above ground) and subterranean shops. The park is built on the site of the iconic Sony Building, which closed in 2018 and is due to reopen after the 2020 Olympics.

OLD IMPERIAL BAR

Continue under the raised expressway and the railway tracks, keeping an eye out for Shinkansen. You will eventually arrive back where you started above Hibiya Station. To round off, there are a couple of choices. You could turn left and follow the track until you reach the junction with Miyuki-dori where to the right is the rear of the **Imperial Hotel**. Pop inside to see the sole remains of Frank Lloyd Wright's original design in the hotel's **Old Imperial Bar** ⓫. For something more rustic, head back towards Yurakucho Station, to the atmospheric tavern **Shin-hinomoto**, see ❹.

Food and drink

❶ PÂTISSERIE SADAHARU AOKI

3-4-1 Marunouchi, Chiyoda-ku; tel: 5293 2800; www.sadaharuaoki.com; daily 11am–8pm; station: Yurakucho; ¥
Pastry chef Sadaharu Aoki is the toast of Paris for his divine sweet creations. Sample éclairs, macaroons and filled croissants here at his first Tokyo 'boutique'.

❷ GGCO. CAFÉ & BAKERY

2-1-3 Kyobashi, Chuo-ku; tel: 3516 9555; www.cytokyo.com; Mon–Fri 7.30am–8pm, Sat 10am–6pm; station: Kyobashi; ¥
Relaxed café on the ground floor of the Courtyard by Marriott hotel, serving a wide range of Italian coffees, black and *matcha* teas, cakes and pastries.

❸ LION BEER HALL

7-9-20 Ginza, Chuo-ku; tel: 3571 2590; www.ginzalion.jp; Mon–Sat 11.30am–11pm, Sun 11.30am–10.30pm; station: Ginza; ¥¥
Worth dropping by, if only to marvel at the ground-floor beer hall's vaulted ceiling and mosaic-lined decor. Brewery Sapporo's beers are accompanied by Germanic-style sausages and the like.

❹ ANDY'S SHIN-HINOMOTO

2-4-4 Yurakucho, Chiyoda-ku; tel: 3214 8021; www.andysfish.com; Mon–Sat 4pm–midnight; stations: Yurakucho or Hibiya; ¥¥
A noisy, friendly, foreign-run no-nonsense *izakaya* (tavern) built under the railway tracks, serving fresh seafood at reasonable prices. English-speaking.

High-end shopping in Tokyo Midtown

ROPPONGI & AKASAKA

Once notorious nightlife districts, both Roppongi and Akasaka have become places to explore during the day for their art galleries and design delights, as well as great shopping and dining opportunities.

> **DISTANCE:** 8km (5 miles)
> **TIME:** A leisurely day
> **START:** Roppongi Station
> **END:** Akasaka Station
> **POINTS TO NOTE:** Don't do this walk on Tuesday if you want to visit the art galleries on the route.

To the southwest of the Imperial Palace, the area of Roppongi, meaning 'six trees', was once a garrison town for the Meiji government. After World War II the American occupation forces established barracks here, giving it its start as the hub of Tokyo's international nightlife. Still infamous for its pick-up and strip bars, the area is undergoing a cultural makeover to become a focus for the city's contemporary art and design scenes, following the success of the upscale Roppongi Hills and Tokyo Midtown complexes, which combine luxury shopping, hotels and restaurants with offices and galleries.

Down the hill, nearby Akasaka is as busy with office workers and politicians by day as it is with restaurant- and bar-goers by night. It's also home to one of the city's most important shrines, as well as the TBS Broadcasting Centre.

ROPPONGI

Emerging from Roppongi Station at exit 4, find your bearings at **Roppongi Crossing** ❶ (Roppongi kosaten). On the other side of the road, under the raised expressway, you will see the pink and white stripes of the Almond Coffee Shop, while to your left along Gaien-Higashi-dori is the Remm Hotel – head in this direction towards the 248m (813ft) Midtown Tower, anchor of the vast Tokyo Midtown development.

Tokyo Midtown

Covering nearly 70,000 sq m (753,470 sq ft), **Tokyo Midtown** ❷ (www.tokyo-midtown.com) is its own elegant world of offices, shops, apartments, a convention centre, two museum-galleries and other public facilities. Behind Midtown Tower you will find the small traditional garden of **Hinokicho Park** (Hinokicho-koen), while throughout the

Roppongi Hills shopping centre

complex are interesting pieces of contemporary sculpture. There's a bewildering array of restaurants and cafés here – for something upmarket try **Miyagawacho Suiren**, see ❶.

Apart from indulging in some shopping or dining, you may wish to spend some time exploring the complex's two museum-galleries.

The focus is on traditional Japanese arts, such as lacquerware, ceramics and textiles, at the small but classy

Suntory Museum of Art ❸ (www.suntory.com/sma; Sun–Mon, Wed–Thu 10am–6pm, Fri–Sat 10am–8pm), in the northern corner of the complex. The building, designed by Kengo Kuma, also has a traditional tea-ceremony room.

The angular construction jutting out of the lawn to the rear of Tokyo Midtown is the **21_21 Design Sight** ❹ (www.2121designsight.jp; Wed–Mon 10am–7pm), the result of a collaboration between architect Ando Tadao

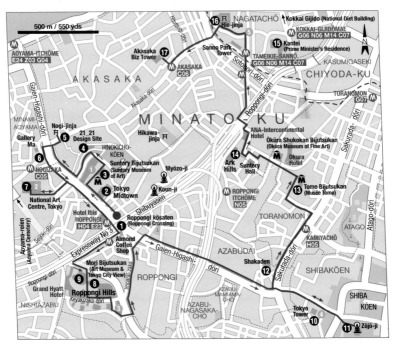

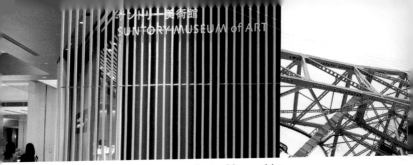

Suntory Museum of Art

and fashion designer Issey Miyake. The main gallery, which is below ground, holds exhibitions on specific themes from a range of designers.

For those with a yen to splurge on a bit of nightlife, Tokyo Midtown is also host to one of Japan's poshest dinner clubs in the form of Billboard Live (http://billboard-live.com). The Tokyo outpost of a nationwide chain, Billboard Live offers acts like jazz great Herbie Hancock against the backdrop of a giant, panoramic window looking out over the night-time downtown skyline.

Nogi-jinja
A five-minute walk north of Tokyo Midtown along Gaien-Higashi-dori, across the road from Nogizaka subway station, is **Nogi-jinja** ❺ (www.nogijinja.or.jp; daily 6am–5pm). The shrine is named after General Nogi Maresuke, a hero of the Russo-Japanese War of 1904, who is buried with his wife—they disembowelled themselves with a sword in solidarity with the death of Emperor Meiji and thus helped to revive ritual suicide in Japan—in nearby Aoyama Cemetery. On the second Sunday of every month an antiques flea market is held in the shrine's grounds.

Gallery Ma
Across the main road, check out what's showing at **Gallery Ma** ❻ (www.toto.co.jp/gallerma; Tue–Sat 11am–6pm), which mounts exhibitions on interior design and architecture from both Japan and overseas; past subjects have

included the likes of Ando Tadao. The gallery is on the third floor of a showroom for Toto, Japan's largest toilet manufacturer, so you can also check out the latest in bathroom design while you are here.

National Art Centre, Tokyo
Retrace your steps along Gaien-Higashi-dori back towards Tokyo Midtown, where you should turn right to reach the wavy glass-wall façade of the **National Art Centre, Tokyo** ❼ (NACT; www.nact.jp; Wed–Mon 10am–6pm). Designed by Kurokawa Kisha, this 48,000-sq m (516,600-sq ft) building is Japan's largest such gallery, staging everything from blockbuster exhibitions of major artists to small-scale shows for local art groups. The atrium foyer is studded with three-storey-tall conical pods – on the top of one you will find **Brasserie Paul Bocuse Le Musée**, see ❷. For unusual souvenirs, look in the shop in the National Art Centre's basement.

Roppongi Hills
Return to Roppongi Crossing, turn right and follow Roppongi-dori towards **Roppongi Hills** ❽ (www.roppongihills.com), a complex that is among the brashest of Tokyo's mini-cities. Its 54-storey tower, deluxe **Grand Hyatt** hotel, nine-screen cinema and over 200 shops form one of the largest developments in Japan. In the plaza outside the entrance to the Mori Tower you will see Louise Bourgeois's *Maman*, an iconic sculpture of

Tokyo Tower · *Art atop the Mori Tower in Roppongi Hills*

a giant spider that has become to Roppongi Hills what Hachiko is to Shibuya.

The top floors of the **Mori Tower** are occupied by the **Mori Art Museum** ❾ (MAM, Mori Bijutsukan; www.mori.art. museum; Tue 10am–5pm, Wed–Mon 10am–10pm), which aspires – and is judged by many to have achieved the goal – to be Japan's leading contemporary art museum. Under the curation of Director Nanjo Fumio, the museum hosts exhibitions of works mainly from Japan and Asia, with a focus on Asia's booming contemporary art market. The Mori underwent an extensive renovation in 2015 and now boasts a number of technological advancements that enable it to better accommodate the growing movement toward multimedia forms of artistic expression. You can combine a visit to the museum with the **Tokyo City View** (Sun–Thu 10am–11pm, Fri–Sat 10am–1am) observation deck, which in recent years hosts unusual Sky Aquarium exhibitions and all-night club events. Weather permitting, it's also fun to go out on the tower's roof to take in the panorama from the **Sky Deck** (daily 10am–8pm).

Return to ground level, exit onto boutique-lined Keyakizaka-dori and take the side road behind the Tsutaya book, CD and DVD store to find the Singaporean restaurant **Hainan Jeefan Shokudo**, see ❸.

Across the road from Tsutaya, turn left then right to follow Imoarai-zaka uphill back towards Roppongi Crossing. Just before reaching there, branch right to emerge on Gaien-Higashi-dori and the heart of Roppongi's main drag of bars and nightclubs.

Tokyo Tower

Keep on walking east along Gaien-Higashi-dori, passing under the raised expressway towards the orange-and-white-painted **Tokyo Tower** ❿ (www. tokyotower.co.jp; daily 9am–11pm). Even though it no longer offers the highest vantage point over the city, it's still worth getting close up to this Tokyo icon to admire its Eiffel Tower-like structure. A gaggle of restaurants and kitschy amusements like theme park exhibits and a mocked-up Shinto shrine can be found in the Foot Town at the base of the tower, where you can also fuel up at **Tango**, see ❹.

Zojo-ji

Adjacent to Tokyo Tower in **Shiba Park** (Shiba-koen) sits one of Tokyo's most impressive temples – **Zojo-ji** ⓫ (www. zojoji.or.jp; daily 9am–5pm). Founded in 1393, the site was chosen by the Tokugawa clan in the late 1600s as their ancestral temple; six of the Tokugawa shoguns are buried here. Close to the bay and the Tokaido (East Sea Road), it also served as a post station for travellers. Most of the temple buildings, once numbering over 100, have not survived the ravages of time, but its main entrance, the 1612 red-lacquered Sanmon, is original. The Main Hall (Taiden) contains ancient sutras and statuary.

Shakaden

Return to Tokyo Tower and turn right on Sakurada-dori to walk towards Kami-yacho subway station, passing the striking **Shakaden 12**. With its enormous, wedge-like black roof it may look like an alien spaceship, but this is the Tokyo headquarters of the Reiyukai Buddhist movement (www.reiyukaiindia.org/shakaden.asp).

Musée Tomo

Walk past the entrances to Kamiyacho Station and turn left, heading uphill towards the Toranomon Tower complex. Walk through this towards the **Okura Hotel** to encounter the **Musée Tomo 13** (Tomo Bijutsukan; 4-1-35 Toranomon, Mina-

to-ku; www.musee-tomo.or.jp; Tue–Sun 11am–6pm), a small but highly elegant museum housing the contemporary Japanese ceramics collection of Tomo Kikuchi.

Head west from the Okura Hotel to arrive at the rear of the **Ark Hills 14** complex, a precursor of Roppongi Hills. Located here are the ANA Intercontinental Hotel and the classical-music venue **Suntory Hall** (www.suntory.com/culture-sports/suntoryhall). You will emerge back on Roppongi-dori facing the raised expressway.

AKASAKA

Kantei

Cross Roppongi-dori to enter Akasaka. Walk towards Tameike-Sanno subway station, near to which you can see the Sanno Park Tower and the handsome residence of Japan's Prime Minister, known as the **Kantei 15**. You can't go inside, but you can take a virtual tour (see www.kantei.go.jp/foreign/vt/index.html). A short distance to the north, Japan's parliament sits in the **National Diet Building** (Kokkai Gijido), a successful blend of Japanese and Western styles that opened in 1936. Those with an interest in Japanese politics can tour the House of Councillors (www.sangiin.go.jp/eng/info/dbt), the upper house of the nation's bicameral parliament.

Hie-jinja

Next to Sanno Park Tower, steps lead up to one of Tokyo's premier shrines – **Hie-jinja 16** (www.hiejinja.net; daily Apr–

High-rise Tokyo

The 333m (1,092ft) tall Tokyo Tower, built in 1958, is still one of the city's tallest structures, even if its top-most observation deck only lets you get up to 250m (820ft). The Mori Tower in Roppongi Hills allows visitors access to its rooftop observation deck at 270m (885ft), while nearby you can sip cocktails and look out of the 248m (814ft) tall Midtown Tower from the lobby of the Ritz-Carlton Hotel. As of 2011, however, all this was dwarfed by the 610m (2001ft) Tokyo Sky Tree (www.tokyo-skytree.jp) in the Narihi-rabashi/Oshiage area, east across the Sumida River from Asakusa; the building's topmost observation point is at the giddy height of 450m (1,475ft).

Statues of the bodhisattva Jizo at Zojo-ji – each is for the soul of a departed child

Sept 5am–6pm, Oct–Mar 6am–5pm). Transplanted to the borders of the Akasaka and Nagatacho districts in the 17th century in the belief that it would help to deflect evil from Edo Castle, the shrine's current buildings were erected in 1967. Its role as protector is still evident today; look carefully at a carving to the left of the main shrine and you will see a monkey cradling its baby. Pregnant women come here to pay homage to the image. Downhill from the shrine, away from the main road, you will find the restaurant **Kurosawa**, see ⑤.

Leave the shrine the way you entered, cross the street and head southwest for a couple of blocks to reach the **Akasaka Biz Tower** ⑰, another of the area's new dining, shopping and business complexes. Nearby is Akasaka Station.

Food and drink

① MIYAGAWACHO SUIREN

3F Garden Terrace, Tokyo Midtown, 9-7-4 Akasaka, Minato-ku; tel: 5413 1881; www. kyoto-suiren.com; Mon–Fri 11am–midnight, Sat–Sun 11am–11pm; station: Roppongi; ¥¥
Exquisitely presented traditional Kyoto cuisine is the order of the day at this smart restaurant, with a menu reflecting the changing of the seasons and availability of fresh ingredients.

② BRASSERIE PAUL BOCUSE LE MUSÉE

National Art Centre, 7-22-2 Roppongi, Minato-ku; tel: 5770 8161; www.paulbocuse.jp/eng/musee; Wed–Mon 11am–7:30pm (L.O) Fri 11am–8:30pm (L.O); station: Roppongi; ¥¥¥
Make a booking if you want to avoid queuing up for lunch at this classy French operation, notable for its location atop one of the giant concrete cones in the Art Centre's lobby.

③ HAINAN JEEFAN SHOKUDO

6-11-16 Roppongi, Minato-ku; tel: 5474 3200; www.route9g.com; Mon–Fri 11.30am–2pm and 6pm–11pm, Sat–Sun 11.30am–3pm and 6–11pm; station: Roppongi; ¥¥
Tasty Singaporean street food, such as chicken rice and spicy noodles, are served up at this cute place near Roppongi Hills.

④ TANGO

3-5-4 Shiba-koen, Minato-ku; tel: 5733 6866; www.tango-tpt.com; Mon–Sat 11.30am–11.30pm, Sun 11.30am–10.30pm; station: Kamiyacho; ¥¥
Enjoy unrivalled views of the Tokyo Tower from this terrace restaurant, which serves a wide-ranging international menu from Italian burrata and prosciutto to Japanese *panko*-coated Pacific saury.

⑤ KUROSAWA

2-7-9 Nagatacho, Chiyoda-ku; tel: 3580 9638; Mon–Fri 11.30am–3pm and 5–11pm, Sat noon–10pm; station: Tameike-sanno; ¥¥
Enjoy gourmet *soba* noodle-and-pork dishes in this atmospheric restaurant that takes its design cues from Akira Kurosawa's movies.

Prada's distinctive shopfront

AOYAMA & HARAJUKU

These two western quarters are known as much for their staid high-end boutiques as for their ceaselessly churning Tokyo street fashions. But you can also find traditional and contemporary art galleries and the city's top Shinto shrine, hidden in a forest that also harbours a beautiful iris garden.

DISTANCE: 5.5km (3.5 miles)
TIME: 6 hours
START: Omotesando Station
END: Kita-Sando or Harajuku stations
POINTS TO NOTE: Almost all the area's boutiques are open from 11am or noon to 8pm, so it's best to start this walk late morning or early afternoon. To see some outrageous costumes, come on a Sunday when *cosplayers* (fans dressed as their favourite *anime* characters or pop idols) hang out around Harajuku Station.

Once a post station on the Kamakura Kaido, a road that ran from the 11th-century imperial capital of Kamakura to the remote northern reaches, Harajuku is now associated with all that is trendy, from streetwear to designer labels, branches of which are clustered along super-stylish Omotesando. At this zelkova tree-lined boulevard's eastern end is the high-fashion district of Aoyama. Here you can view some stunning examples of modern architecture.

AOYAMA

From exit A4 of Omotesando Station you'll emerge at the narrow end of Omotesando near the boutiques of some of Japan's top fashion talent, such as **Issey Miyake** (3-18-11 Minami-Aoyama, Minato-ku; www.isseymiyake.com), **Yohji Yamamoto** (5-3-6 Minami-Aoyama; www.yohjiyamamoto.co.jp) and Kawakubo Rei, designer for **Comme des Garçons** (5-2-1 Minami-Aoyama). The most striking boutique is **Prada ❶** (5-2-6 Minami-Aoyama), in a giant bubble-wrapped glass structure designed by architects Jacques Herzog and Pierre de Meuron.

Japanese design strikes back towards the end of the street at **La Collezione ❷**, a work by Pritzker Prize-winning architect Ando Tadao, where shops and offices are housed within a cylinder of concrete.

Nezu Museum of Art

At the end of Omotesando is the **Nezu Museum of Art ❸** (Nezu Bijutsu-kan; www.nezu-muse.or.jp; Tue–Sun 10am–4.30pm), with its ceramics, textiles, calligraphy, paintings and tea-ceremony utensils. Among its treasures are the

Entrance to Meiji Jingu Shinto shrine

Kamakura-period Nanchi Waterfall scroll painting and Ogata Korin's *Irises* (only displayed in the last week of April and early May). The elegant, Kengo Kuma-designed museum's sloping garden, with its pond, teahouse and stupas, is a gem.

Return to the main Omotesando crossing, perhaps pausing for refreshments at the elegant café and confectioner's **Yoku Moku**, see ❶.

HARAJUKU

Walk northwest along Omotesando, heading into Harajuku; halfway down the boulevard's main section, on the right-

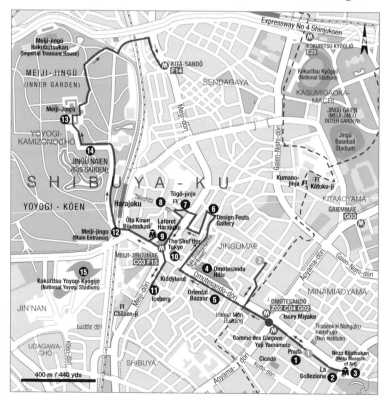

Barrels of sake brought for blessing at Meiji–jingu

hand side, you will find Ando Tadao's second contribution – **Omotesando Hills** ❹ (www.omotesandohills.com). This complex of shops and apartments deliberately stays beneath the treeline outside, while inside it burrows deep into the ground to create a striking central atrium encircled by a spiralling walkway that replicates the angle and incline of the pavement. There are several places to eat and drink here, but also worth searching out on the backstreets to the northeast is the venerable *tonkatsu* restaurant **Maisen**, see ❷.

Across the road, you can't miss the mock-traditional architecture of the red-and-green-painted **Oriental Bazaar** ❺ (5-9-13 Jingumae, Shibuya-ku; www.orientalbazaar.co.jp), a large traditional crafts and furnishings shop targeted at the foreign buyer. On the upper floors you will find a decent selection of genuine antiques. Nearby is recently renovated **Kiddyland** (6-1-9 Jingumae, Shibuya-ku; www.kiddyland.co.jp), one of the city's best toy stores.

Design and shrines

Across the road from Kiddyland is **Cat Street**, packed with emerging boutiques that provide a youthful counterpoint to the adult sophistication of Omotesando. Stroll north along it until you reach the entrance to **Design Festa Gallery** ❻ (www.designfestagallery.com; daily 11am–8pm), a colourful explosion of contemporary art galleries based in several old houses and an apartment block.

Work your way west towards Meiji-dori and the main entrance to the shrine

Togo-jinja ❼. An excellent antiques and flea market is held in the grounds of the shrine on the first and fourth Sunday of the month from 8am to around 2pm.

Cutting-edge shopping

Exit Togo-jinja's grounds directly into the consumer mayhem of **Takeshita-dori** ❽, a narrow pedestrian street packed with cheap fashion, jewellery and knick-knack stores as well as outlets selling merchandise associated with Japan's idol groups that are constantly thronged with teenagers; at weekends this may well be the most densely crowded place in the city. A right turn leads you to the Takeshita entrance of Harajuku Station, while a left turn brings you back to the relative calm of Meiji-dori.

Continue past Takeshita-dori and find on the right **Laforet Harajuku** ❾ (1-11-6 Jingumae; www.laforet.ne.jp/en/; daily 11am–9pm), a small but fashionable department store crammed with some of Tokyo's hippest boutiques and a small but keenly curated museum on the top floor often featuring works by some of Japan's most cutting-edge artists and designers. Opposite Laforet on the northeast corner of the intersection of Meiji-dori and Omotosando lies **The Shel'tter Tokyo** ❿ (4-30-3 Jingumae; www.sheltter.jp/tokyo; daily 11am–9pm, another opulent new edifice of consumerism, with yet more trendy shops and a rooftop garden and café.

Cross Omotesando to the south and continue along Meiji-dori until you hit, on

Kiddyland kitsch

the left, the **Iceberg** (6-12-8 Jingu-mae), formerly known as the Audi Forum. Designed by British architect Benjamin Warner, this multi-faceted glass building looks like a giant crystal shard.

Ota Memorial Museum of Art

Return to Omotesando, turn left uphill and take the first lane on the right when you see a branch of Muji to find the excellent **Ota Memorial Museum of Art** (Ota Kinen Bijutsukan; 1-10-10 Jingumae, Shibuya-ku; www.ukiyoe-ota-muse.jp; Tue–Sun 10.30am–5pm). The galleries feature monthly selections from a body of more than 12,000 *ukiyo-e* woodblock prints, many by masters of the genre like Hiroshige, Utamaru and Hokusai.

Alternatively, return to Omotesando and head uphill to reach the main mock-Tudor entrance to Harajuku Station, built in 1924. Cross the bridge over the tracks and bear right. A huge cypress torii gate announces the main entrance to **Meiji-jingu** (www.meijijingu.or.jp), Tokyo's premier Shinto shrine, deifying the emperor Meiji, who died in 1912. This is the Inner Garden; the Outer Garden is around 1km (0.6 mile) to the east and contains several sports stadia. The main shrine buildings are about 1km (0.6 mile) from the entrance along a broad gravel path through a forest.

On the left, just before you turn into Meiji-jingu's central complex, is the entrance to the **Jingu Naien** (daily 8.30am–5pm). In June crowds flock to this lush garden, with an old teahouse overlooking a lily pond, to see around 100 different species of iris bloom.

Yoyogi Park

If you leave by the northern gate, the nearest subway station is Kita-Sando on Meiji-dori. Otherwise return to the Harajuku exit and, if you desire more open space, pop into the neighbouring **Yoyogi Park** (Yoyogi-koen), one of the city's best spots for people-watching, particularly in the hanami season. Also take a moment to admire the fluid lines of concrete tents and pavilions that make up Kenzo Tange's **National Yoyogi Stadium** .

Food and drink

① YOKU MOKU

5-3-3 Minami-Aoyama, Minato-ku; tel: 5485 3330; www.yokumoku.co.jp; Mon–Sat 10am–11pm, Sun 10am–7pm; station: Omotesando; ¥

Famous for its crisp, wafer-thin rolled biscuits, this blue-tiled café is an elegant place for refreshments, of which you partake in an outdoor courtyard.

② MAISEN

4-8-5 Jingumae, Shibuya-ku; tel: 3470 0071; http://mai-sen.com; daily 11am–10pm; station: Omotesando; ¥¥

This well-regarded *tonkatsu* (deep-fried breaded pork cutlets) restaurant, based in a former bathhouse, also serves deep-fried chicken and oysters. English menu available.

SHIBUYA & EBISU

This walk through the teen-trend Mecca of Shibuya and neighbouring district of Ebisu has something for everyone, including shopaholics, kids and lovers of quirky museums and contemporary art.

> **DISTANCE:** 4km (2.5 miles)
> **TIME:** 4–6 hours
> **START:** Shibuya Station
> **END:** Ebisu Station
> **POINTS TO NOTE:** This walk can be combined with Aoyama and Harajuku (route 4) by catching the train or subway to Shibuya or walking about 10 minutes between the two areas. The best time is towards the late afternoon to see Shibuya in its neon-lit brilliance.

As late as the 1880s, tea plantations covered the slopes that surround the valley known as Shibuya, but the area is now undergoing a dramatic transformation that is changing the station environs from a low-rise district into a nest of visionary skyscrapers. As with Shinjuku and Ikebukuro, the coming of the railways, and the department stores attached to them, changed all that. Today, this vibrant entertainment and shopping district is one of the most exciting in Tokyo, the centre from which fashion trends ripple out to

the rest of Japan. This walk also takes you to the neighbouring area of Ebisu, named after a Shinto god of good fortune and the site of a one-time brewery now morphed into a complex of shops, restaurants and cultural facilities.

SHIBUYA

Several train and subway lines converge on Shibuya Station. From wherever you arrive, make your way through the Tokyu Toyoko department store towards the western side, which houses the terminus for the Keio-Inokashira line (you can hop on this later to visit the Japan Folk Crafts Museum). On the way you will pass a giant 14-panel painting, **Myth of Tomorrow** ❶ *(Asu no Shinwa)* by Okamoto Taro (1911–96), a powerful *Guernica*-like mural of the atomic-bomb explosion. Originally created in the late 1960s for a luxury hotel in Mexico, the monumental work was rediscovered in 2003 and took five years to be restored and find its new home in the station.

Statue of Hachiko and his master

Hachiko Statue

Out of the window facing the Okamoto mural you will have a good view over **Shibuya Crossing** (Shibuya Kosaten), a mesmerising confluence of neon, giant video screens and endless streams of people. Emerge at ground level in the plaza outside the station and dig among the crowds to find the statue of the faithful dog **Hachiko ❷**, one of Tokyo's most famous meeting spots.

An Akita breed, Hachiko belonged to a Tokyo University professor who lived in Shibuya in the 1920s. The dog accompanied him to the station each morning, and met him there promptly every evening. When the professor died in 1925, Hachiko continued turning up to the station for the next decade until her own death, earning the affection of locals for exemplifying loyalty to a master.

Tokyo Wonder Site

One block north, you'll find a gallery that's part of the **Tokyo Wonder Site ❸** (www.tokyoartsandspace.jp; Tue–Sun 11am–7pm). Always worth a look inside, the project is dedicated to the generation and promotion of contemporary art and culture in Tokyo.

Interesting shops

Cross Koen-dori and walk between the fashion stores **Parco Part II** and Parco Part I towards **Tokyu Hands ❹** (www.tokyu-hands.co.jp; daily 10am–9pm) on the left. This home-improvements and hobbies store is a great place for souvenirs, creative materials and outdoor goods of all kinds.

Head southwest towards Bunkamura-dori to find the main Tokyu department store and the attached arts centre **Bunkamura ❺** (www.bunkamura.co.jp). Meaning 'culture village', the complex offers art galleries, a cinema, a theatre and the 2,150-seat **Orchard Hall**, an acoustically excellent shoe-box-style hall used for

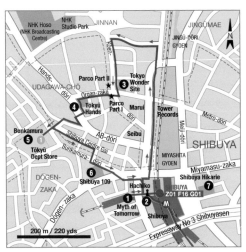

Relaxing in Yebisu Garden Place

classical-music concerts. Also here is **Les Deux Magots**, see .

Shibuya 109

Running parallel to the north of Bunka-mura-dori is narrow Centre Gai, a pedestrian street that acts as a catwalk of the latest Shibuya fashion. Having picked out some ideas, proceed to the distinctive silver silo of **Shibuya 109** ❻ (2-29-1 Dogenzaka, Shibuya-ku; www.shibuya109.jp; daily 10am–9pm) at the apex of Bunkamori-dori and Dogenzaka. This Shibuya landmark embodies the trends and culture of the teenage girls who play a leading role in Japanese consumer culture. Even if you don't fit into the targeted demographic, just walking through the countless boutiques filled with young fashionistas

and echoing with dance music is quite an adventure.

This street is named after the highway robber Dogen who once waylaid travellers on this slope *(zaka)*. Walking away from Shibuya Station up Dogenzaka, to the right you will find an area dense with love hotels – the rent-by-the-hour places patronised by Tokyo couples looking for a little privacy.

Shibuya Hikarie

Shibuya's latest landmark retail complex, **Hikarie** ❼ (2-21-1 Shibuya, Shibuya-ku; www.hikarie.jp; daily 11am–11pm) is a vast and glistening warren of trendy boutiques, cafes and restaurants, with the giant Tokyu Theatre Orb (devoted to musicals) suspended midway up its concrete and glass girth. It's best accessed via a suspended walkway from the east side of Shibuya Station.

EBISU

Return to Shibuya Station and take the JR Yamanote line one stop south to **Ebisu**. A moving walkway links the station with **Yebisu Garden Place** ❽ (www.gardenplace.jp), built on the site of the old Sapporo brewery. The spacious complex includes shops, restaurants, the Westin Hotel, a 39-storey tower, a cinema, a performance hall and a mock-French chateau housing a Joël Robuchon restaurant.

Japan Folk Crafts Museum

The outstanding Japan Folk Crafts Museum (Mingei-kan; 4-3-33 Komaba, Meguro-ku; www.mingeikan.or.jp; Tue–Sun 10am–5pm) is located two stops from Shibuya on the Keio-Inokashira line. Alight at Komaba-Todaimae Station and walk northwest for a couple of minutes to find the lovely old building constructed of wood and stone, and once owned by master potter Yanagi Soetsu. A variety of ceramics, furniture and textiles are exhibited in this shrine to *mingei*, Japan's folk-craft movement.

Two museums

Learn about the brewery that used to be here at the **Museum of Yebisu Beer** (www.sapporobeer.jp/brewery; Tue–Sun 11am–7pm), which includes a virtual-reality tour that explains aspects of the brewing process and an opportunity to sample some of Sapporo's beers at Tasting Salon (charge).

On the complex's western side is the superb **Tokyo Photographic Art Museum** (Tokyo-to Shashin Bijut-sukan; http://topmuseum.jp; Tue–Sun 10am–6pm, Thu–Fri until 8pm), the city's premier exhibition space for notable photography and video art. The museum reopened after extensive renovations in 2016.

Before leaving Yebisu Garden Place you could grab something to eat at **Chibo**, see ②, on the 38th floor of the tower. Alternatively, return to Ebisu Station, just northwest of which you will find delicious grilled chicken and sake at **Ebisu Imaiya**, see ③.

Food and drink

① LES DEUX MAGOTS
2-24-1 Dogenzaka, Shibuya-ku; tel: 3477 9124; www.bunkamura.co.jp; daily 11.30am–10.30pm; station: Shibuya; ¥
Wind down over a cup of coffee or a glass of wine at this branch of the famous Parisian café-bistro inside the Bunkamura arts complex.

② CHIBO
38F Yebisu Garden Place Tower, 4-20-3 Ebisu, Shibuya-ku; tel: 5424 1011; Mon–Fri 11.30am–2.30pm and 5–11pm, Sat–Sun 11.30am–11pm; station: Ebisu; ¥¥
Okonomiyaki (savoury pancakes) are made before your eyes on grills set in the table. Fun food and never expensive, plus a brilliant view.

③ EBISU IMAIYA
1-7-11 Ebisu-Nishi, Shibuya-ku; tel: 5456 0255; Mon–Thu 5pm–2am, Fri 5pm–4am, Sat and Sun 5pm–midnight; station: Ebisu; ¥¥
Delectable free-range chicken, served either as *yakitori* (charcoal-grilled) or in warming hotpots. Spotless and efficient, and everything is explained in English.

SHINJUKU

Split by Japan's busiest station, one side of Shinjuku is dominated by sky-high architecture, the other by shops and a neon-festooned entertainment area — a sometimes seedy, but enthralling legacy of Tokyo's old pleasure districts.

DISTANCE: 8km (5 miles)
TIME: A leisurely day
START: Tochomae Station
END: Shinjuku Station
POINTS TO NOTE: Save yourself the hassle of working out which of the hundreds of exits from Shinjuku Station to take by alighting instead at Tochomae, the subway stop closest to the Tokyo Metropolitan Government Office. Note the early closing time of Shinjuku Garden (last entry at 4pm).

A microcosm of Tokyo, Shinjuku offers soaring high-rises, massive malls, tiny shops, classy boutiques, a beautiful and spacious garden and a maze of entertainment venues. The district is home to infamous Kabukicho, Japan's largest red-light district, but just a short stroll away is the imposing Tokyo Metropolitan Government Office. The area is a fertile ground for shopping, dining, people-watching and simply taking in all that is contemporary Japan.

A thick band of railway lines splits the district, west of the centre, into Nishi (West) and Higashi (East) Shinjuku.

WEST SHINJUKU

If you haven't emerged from Tochomae Station in West Shinjuku, then orientate yourself towards the western exit of Shinjuku Station and the fountains at the centre of the sunken plaza just in front of Odakyu department store. An underground walkway beneath Chuo-dori runs from here to the first sight.

TOKYO METROPOLITAN GOVERNMENT OFFICE

Designed by award-winning architect Kenzo Tange, the **Tokyo Metropolitan Government Office ❶** (also known as the **Tocho**) is the city's governmental nerve centre. Its monumental yet elegant design, with twin 48-storey towers, makes it stand out amid a grove of fellow skyscrapers at the end of Chuo-dori.

Omoide Yokocho is lined with food stalls

Head up to the 45th floor of either tower to take in the panoramic view from the **Observation Rooms** (www.metro.tokyo.jp; daily 9.30am–11pm). On a clear day you will be rewarded with a panorama that stretches from Mount Fuji to the hills of the Boso Peninsula in Chiba Prefecture. You can also take a 40-minute tour of the complex (Mon–Fri 10am–3pm), departing from the **Tokyo Tourist Information Centre** on the ground floor. Cross over to the scrappy Shinjuku Chuo Park (Shinjuku Chuo-koen), from where you can get a good view of the Tocho's exterior design.

Shinjuku Park Tower

Immediately south of the park stands another Tange building, the Postmodernist, 52-storey **Shinjuku Park Tower ②**. The three stylish linked towers, with their luminous glass pyramids, house the luxurious Park Hyatt Hotel and its glamorous **New York Grill** restaurant, see ①. Also here are a number of floors devoted to interior design and architecture, including the first-rate **Living Design Centre Ozone** (www.ozone.co.jp/eng; Thu–Tue 10.30am–7pm), which has exhibitions relating to modern interior design.

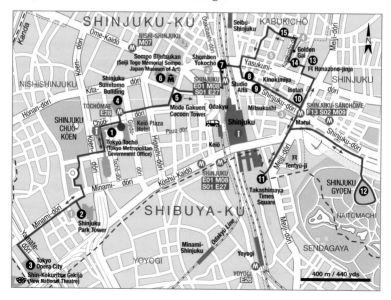

The Cocoon Tower

Tokyo Opera City

It's a 10-minute stroll west of the tower along Minami-dori to **Tokyo Opera City** ❸ (www.operacity.jp/en), a 54-floor complex of shops, offices and restaurants. There's an **art gallery** (Tue–Thu 11am–7pm, Fri–Sat 11am–8pm) and a **concert hall** here, but you are likely to find the most interesting part of the complex to be the **NTT Intercommunication Centre** (www.ntticc.or.jp; Tue–Sun 11am–6pm), an interactive, high-tech exhibition space, with an electronic library and internet café. Also part of the complex is the **New National Theatre** (www.nntt.jac.go.jp), housing opera, theatre and modern dance venues.

Sumitomo Building

Return the way you came to Chuo-dori. Opposite the Tocho is the **Sumitomo Building** ❹. This six-sided construction's atrium stretches from the fourth to the 52nd floor. In case you didn't make it up the Tocho (or just want another bird's-eye view), there's also a free observatory here on the 51st floor.

Mode Gakuen Cocoon Tower

Walk east along Chuo-dori towards the ultra-contemporary, cross-hatched **Mode Gakuen Cocoon Tower** ❺, one of the most striking new additions to the Shinjuku skyline. Designed by Tange Associates, and occupied by a fashion and computer-studies school, this 50-storey glass stunner has a large bookstore, **Book 1st** (www.book1st.net), in its basement; the store includes Tokyo Magazine Centre, stocking some 5,000 titles from around the world.

Seiji Togo Memorial Sompo Japan Museum of Art

One final skyscraper to check out is the Sompo Japan Building behind Mode Gakuen Cocoon Tower on Kita-dori; on the 42nd floor is the **Seiji Togo Memorial Sompo Japan Museum of Art** ❻ (www.sjnk-museum.org; Tue–Sun 10am–5.30pm). Apart from a collection of stylised works by painter Togo Seiji (1897–1978), you can also view one of Vincent van Gogh's *Sunflowers* and other Impressionist paintings by Cézanne and Gauguin.

Shomben Yokocho

Head east to Shinjuku Station, passing between the bus terminal and the Odakyu Halc Building, and crossing over the road to discover a cluttered, run-down four-block neighbourhood called **Shomben Yokocho** ❼ ('Piss Alley'), hung with red lanterns and packed with friendly hole-in-the-wall restaurants and bars. It's a great place to return to in the evening for inexpensive *yakitori* (grilled chicken) and beers. On the southwestern corner of the district you will find the appealing **Tajimaya Coffee House**, see ❷.

Shinjuku-dori

EAST SHINJUKU

Take a right out of the café and pass a row of discount clothes shops to find a pedestrian tunnel running under the tracks that slice Shinjuku down the middle. You will emerge on the eastern side of the station beside the plaza fronting **Studio Alta** ❽, marked by a giant external video screen – there's always a crowd here, as this is one of the area's most popular meeting spots.

Shinjuku-dori

Turn away from the station and walk along **Shinjuku-dori** ❾, the district's premier shopping street. On the left you will find the original flagship of **Kinokuniya**, one of the city's best bookshops, with a good selection of English titles; on the right are the department stores Mitsukoshi and Marui. Take the road between these two stores to find the esteemed tempura restaurant **Tsunahachi**, see ❸.

Occupying a block on the corner of Meiji-dori and Shinjuku-dori is the department store **Isetan** ❿ (www.isetan.co.jp; daily 10am–8pm), Shinjuku's only major building to have survived from the pre-war period. This chic seven-floor emporium has a connected eight-floor Men's Building to the rear, a fabulous basement food hall, a floor devoted to restaurants and a rooftop garden.

Takashimaya Times Square

Follow Meiji-dori south, crossing Koshu Kaido to reach one of Shinjuku's more modern shopping complexes, **Takashimaya Times Square** ⓫, next to the Shin-Minami entrance to Shinjuku Station. As well as a branch of the eponymous Takashimaya store, you will find **Tokyu Hands**, an innovative handicrafts and interior-design store, and the main branch of the bookstore **Kinokuniya**.

Shinjuku National Garden

East Shinjuku is not all about shopping. From Takashimaya Times Square, return to the crossroads of Koshu Kaido and Meiji-dori, and turn right to reach the main entrance of **Shinjuku National Garden** ⓬ (Shinjuku Gyoen; www.env.go.jp/garden/shinjukugyoen; Tue–Sun 9am–4.30pm, last entry 4pm; Mar–Sep until 6pm, last entry 5.30pm; Jul–Aug until 7pm, last entry 6.30pm). The lovely 60ha (150-acre) grounds, once part of the estate of the *daimyo* (feudal lord) Naito during the Edo period, only opened to the public in 1949. The park is divided into three sections: a northern section containing a garden in the formal French manner; a landscaped English garden at the centre; and a traditional Japanese garden, with winding paths, arched bridges, stone lanterns and artificial hills, in the southern section. Look out for the Taiwan-kaku Pavilion, a Chinese-style gazebo built to commemorate the wedding of the emperor

Kabukicho

Hirohito in 1927. The park's botanical greenhouse has recently been renovated and contains some splendid subtropical plants.

Hanazono-jinja

Retrace your steps to Isetan, walk along its eastern flank down Meiji-dori until you reach the wide boulevard called Yasukuni-dori. Cross it and turn left. Immediately on your right you will see the narrow entrance to the shrine **Hanazono-jinja** ⑬, an oasis of calm at the edge of one of Tokyo's raunchiest entertainment and red-light areas. The shrine dates back to the 6th century, but the current concrete-and-granite structure is more recent. One of the ubiquitous Inari fox shrines (Inari being a major fox deity and also messenger to Ebisu, the god of business and commerce), Hanazono is popular with local shopkeepers, who come here to pray for success in business. The vermillion-and-gold interior of the main hall is impressive. Stone lamps and spotlights come on at night, creating an enchanting atmosphere. A **flea market** is held in the grounds every Sunday.

Golden Gai

Shinjuku has a relationship with alcohol not unlike that of Venice with water: it's built on it. Right next door to the shrine, forming a warren of narrow alleys with a grid of tiny two-storey bars, is **Golden Gai** ⑭ (www.goldengai.net), an endearing, retro crevice of Tokyo saved, for the time being, from the clutches of the speculator. Each of the some 200 bars in this area has a different clientele and most have a cover charge, to dissuade non-regulars, of anything from ¥2,000 to ¥4,000. One that is affordable is **Albatross G**, see ❹; it's in the middle of the fifth alley from the southern end of Golden Gai.

New lodgings

Shinjuku came into existence because of its position at the junction of two key arteries leading into the city from the west. Shinjuku means 'new lodgings', a reference to a post station built on Koshu Kaido for horses and travellers on their way to Edo in the early 18th century.

Trains first rolled into Shinjuku in 1885. The major factor in its rise, however, was its narrow escape from the 1923 Great Kanto Earthquake. Huge numbers of residents moved in, followed by department stores, theatres and artists' studios. The area's importance made it a target for American bombing, which levelled the entire district on 25 May 1945. Yet by the 1970s it had rebounded with West Shinjuku sprouting a gaggle of skyscrapers (such as the Mode Gakuen Cocoon Tower) that, in a generally low-rise city, still remain striking.

Shinjuku National Garden

Kabukicho

An attractive pedestrian pathway skirts the western side of Golden Gai to emerge just a few steps to the right of Kuyakusho-dori in the heart of **Kabukicho**. Tame-looking by day, Kabukicho undergoes a transformation at twilight, when seedy hostess bars, strip joints, porno flea-pits, peep-shows and brothels (innoc-uously named 'Soaplands') spark into neon-lit action. Perhaps the area's most famous attraction is the kitschy, slightly sexy electric extrava-ganza that is **Robot Restaurant** ⑤. Should you be in the mood, splurge on this only-in-Kabukicho experience before heading back a few blocks south across Yasukuni-dori to Shin-juku Station.

Food and drink

① NEW YORK GRILL

52F Park Hyatt Hotel, 3-7-1-2 Nishi-Shinjuku, Shinjuku-ku; tel: 5323 3458; daily 11.30am–2.30pm, 5.30–10pm; station: Tochomae; ¥¥¥¥

Dine in a sky-view setting at Shinjuku's Park Hyatt Hotel (the setting for the film *Lost in Translation*). Sunday brunch with cocktails at the adjacent New York Bar is an institution for the expat community.

② TAJIMAYA COFFEE HOUSE

Shomben Yokocho, Shinjuku-eki Nishi-guchi, Shinjuku-ku; tel: 3342 0881; http://tajimaya-coffeeten.com; daily 10am–10.30pm; station: Shinjuku; ¥

Retreat from the crowds swarming through Shinjuku Station at this warm, wood-furnished establishment on the corner of the first set of alleys here. The café serves a first-rate brew and nice cakes.

③ TSUNAHACHI

3-31-8 Shinjuku, Shinjuku-ku; tel: 3352 1012; www.tunahachi.co.jp; daily 11am–10pm; ¥¥¥; station: Shinjuku

Hearty tempura (deep-fried battered seafood and vegetables) in large portions in an atmospheric wooden building. Good value and busy.

④ ALBATROSS G

2F 5th Ave, 1-1 Kabukicho, Shinjuku-ku; tel: 3202 3699; www.alba-s.com; Mon–Sat 8pm–5am; ¥¥; station: Shinjuku-Sanchome

There's a ¥500 cover charge at this welcoming Golden Gai bar that's the sister operation of a slightly larger Albatross in Shomben Yokocho.

⑤ ROBOT RESTAURANT

1-7-7 Kabukicho, Shinjuku-ku; tel: 3200 5500; www.shinjuku-robot.com/pc; daily 5–11pm; station: Shinjuku-Sanchome

A spectacular hi-tech robot show, fronted by sexy female dancers, transports patrons to another world.

Ueno Park

YANAKA & UENO

On this walk through part of Tokyo's Shitamachi, or 'low city', Yanaka's atmospheric cemetery and Ameyoko's old black-market alleys sandwich the rich cultural attractions of Ueno Park, including the Tokyo National Museum.

DISTANCE: 7.25km (4.5 miles)
TIME: A full day
START: Nippori Station
END: Ueno Station
POINTS TO NOTE: Ueno Park's museums could easily swallow up a day, so if you want to cover the rest of the walk, plan accordingly. Avoid doing this walk on Monday if you want to visit the museums, as this is when most of them are closed.

One of the few Tokyo districts to have come relatively unscathed through both the Great Kanto Earthquake of 1923 and the fire bombings of 1945, Yanaka has somehow also managed to avoid merciless redevelopment in the late 20th and early 21st centuries. This charmingly old-fashioned quarter, north of the Imperial Palace, dates from the Tokugawa Shogunate's decision to fortify the city's periphery with temples that would double as fortresses in the event of invasion.

Ueno Hill, where the giant temple Kan'ei-ji once stood, is now home to Ueno Park and several museums, including the outstanding Tokyo National Museum. The construction of a major railway terminus here in 1883 led to the arrival of millions of migrants from Japan's northeastern provinces in the post-war decades, resulting in a lively multicultural quarter.

YANAKA CEMETERY AND ENVIRONS

Take the western exit from Nippori Station and follow the steps immediately on the left up to **Yanaka Cemetery ❶** (Yanaka Reien), one of the city's oldest graveyards, with mossy tombstones, leafy walks, wrought-iron gates and worn stone lanterns.

Follow the stone path ahead until you reach the twin ancient wood and modern cement-and-steel gates to **Tenno-ji ❷**, a temple dating from the late 14th century. In its grounds you will find a serene-looking copper statue of Buddha crafted in 1690.

Asakura Choso Museum

Follow the main road south through the cemetery, turning right at the first cross-

Ameyoko Street

roads to exit the grounds. At the T-junction beside the temple **Choan-ji**, turn right and follow the road until you reach, on the right,

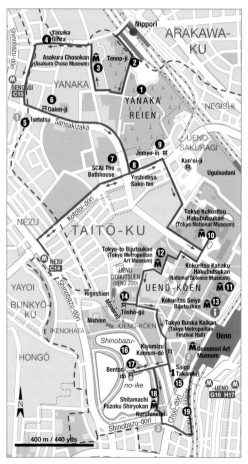

the **Asakura Choso Museum ❸** (Asakura Chosokan; 7-18-10 Yanaka, Taito-ku; Tue–Thu, Sat–Sun 9.30am–4.30pm), an excellent gallery dedicated to the artist Asakura Fumio (1883–1964), often described as the father of modern Japanese sculpture. The museum is based in Asakura's lovely studio-house, dating from 1935. The traditional garden to the rear of the house is of special interest, as stones around the pond have been arranged to reflect the Five Confucian Virtues, while the roof-garden provides panoramic views of the surrounding area.

Yanaka Ginza

Turn right out of the museum, then turn left at the junction with the road that runs back towards Nippori Station. Ahead, to the right of a fork in the road where there is a poodle parlour, a flight of steps leads down to the **Yanaka Ginza ❹**, a narrow shopping street with a retro atmosphere, full of small shops, cafés and traditional crafts stores.

Admiring art at the Tokyo National Museum

ALONG SANSAKIZAKA

At the end of Yanaka Ginza turn left and continue until the next major junction with Sansakizaka. Turn left here and head uphill to find, on the right, one of Tokyo's oldest and most exquisite paper-art shops, **Isetatsu** ❺ (2-18-9 Yanaka, Taito-ku; daily 10am–6pm), specialising in *chiyogami* – printed designs reproduced from original samurai textiles. Here you will find well-crafted fans, combs, dolls and colourful chests of drawers, all handmade from Japanese *washi* paper.

Daien-ji

Opposite Isetatsu and set back from the street is **Daien-ji** ❻, a temple that contains a monument to the charms of Osen, a teashop girl used by the artist Harunobu as a model for several of his woodblock prints. A statue of Kannon, the goddess of mercy, stands next to Osen's monument, and many Tokyoites, especially the elderly, make pilgrimages here to rub a spot on the statue that corresponds to the part of their body where they are suffering an ache or pain in the hope of a cure. If the more worn patches on this statue are anything to go by, stomach ailments and headaches are the most common complaints among Tokyo's senior citizens.

SCAI The Bathhouse

Continue up Sansakizaka until you reach Yanaka Cemetery again. Turn right and follow the road downhill to

SCAI The Bathhouse ❼ (www.scaithe bathhouse.com; Tue–Sat noon–6pm) on the right. The current building, dating from 1951, has been a contemporary art gallery since 1993; for some 200 years before that, it was where the locals came to scrub and soak.

Yoshidaya Sake-ten

At the end of the road on the left is another evocative remnant of Tokyo's past, the **Yoshidaya Sake-ten** ❽ (Tue–Sun 9.30am–4.30pm). This merchant's shop, made from wood and dating from 1910, has been preserved as a museum just like it was in its heyday, with nostalgic posters, giant glass flasks and wooden barrels.

Turn right here and continue towards Nezu Station, about a five-minute walk down Kototoi-dori. Just on the left before reaching the station, take the side road to reach the entrance to the historic restaurant **Hantei**, see ❶.

JOMYO-IN

Backtrack from Hantei up Kototoi-dori until you eventually reach the temple **Jomyo-in** ❾ on the left; you will be greeted by a 20,000-strong army of tiny Jizo figures. A minor incarnation of the Buddha, Jizo is revered in Japan as a deity – the god of health and healing as well as protector of children. He is recognisable all over the country by his red-and-white bib and, in the case of the Jomyo-in, sponge gourds held in the left hand. Jizo statues

Paper-art shop, Isetatsu

Cherry blossom photography at Ueno Park

are continually donated to the temple in the hope that one day they will reach their target of 84,000.

UENO PARK

Tokyo National Museum

A short walk along the road almost opposite the Jomyo-in carries you to the northwestern perimeter of **Ueno Park** (Ueno-koen). Here, the star attraction is the **Tokyo National Museum** ❿ (Tokyo Kokuritsu Hakubutsukan; www.tnm.jp; Tue–Sun 9.30am–5pm, Apr–Dec Fri until 8pm, Apr–Sept Sat–Sun until 6pm), containing the most extensive collection of Japanese art in the world. The museum consists of four main galleries housed within buildings of various styles, including classic Japanese, ferro-concrete and European Beaux Arts. The central building, called the **Honkan**, contains the main permanent collection, a fine display of paintings, ceramics, lacquerware, calligraphy and textiles. Look out for *Pine Grove by the Seashore*, a six-panel gold-leaf screen from the 16th-century Muromachi period, and the consummate brush painting *Pine Trees* by the 16th-century artist Hasegawa Tohaku.

Leave time to explore the west gallery, the **Heisei-kan**, where there are archaeological relics such as funerary *haniwa* statues and, from the Jomon period, bug-eyed clay figures called *dogu*; and also the **Horyu-ji Homotsu-kan**, a newer hall containing priceless treasures from the Horyu-ji, a temple in Nara.

National Museum of Nature and Science

In addition to the newer Miraikan in Odaiba, the venerable **National Museum of Nature and Science** ⓫ (Kokuritsu Kagaku Hakubutsu-kan; www.kahaku.go.jp; Tue–Thu, Sun 9am–5pm, Fri–Sat 9am–8pm) is the second of the capital's two major science museums. Though much of its excellent collection is introduced with Japanese text only, one doesn't need to understand the copy to enjoy exhibitions of dinosaur fossils, or the Japanese space agency's *Hayabusa*, which became the first unmanned spacecraft to land on an asteroid in 2005.

> ## Famous graves
>
> Among the some 7,000 graves at Yanaka Cemetery are those of several distinguished figures. At the graveyard offices (daily 8.30am–5.15pm) attendants will provide a map (in Japanese) and direct you to the last resting places of the composer and blind *koto*-player Miyagi Michio (1894–1956), the botanist Dr Makino Tomitaro (1862–1957), the well-known artist Yokoyama Taikan (1868–1958) and the female murderer Takahashi Oden (1848–79). Japan's last shogun, Tokugawa Yoshinobu (1837–1913), is buried here too, alongside the ignominious and destitute whose unclaimed bodies were once requisitioned by Tokyo University as teaching aids for their medical faculty.

Statue of Saigo Takamori

Two art museums

A short stroll south across the park takes you to the **Tokyo Metropolitan Art Museum** ⑫ (Tokyo-to Bijutsukan; www. tobikan.jp; daily 9am–5pm), where more than 2,600 works of mostly contemporary art are displayed in a light and spacious, partially underground, red-brick building. It is the work of architect Kunio Maekawa, who also designed the **Tokyo Metropolitan Festival Hall** (Tokyo Bunka Kaikan), where music concerts are held, and part of the **National Museum of Western Art** ⑬ (Kokuritsu Seiyo Bijutsukan; www. nmwa.go.jp; Tue–Sun 9.30am–5pm, Fri and Sat until 8pm); both are on the park's eastern side. The original part of the Museum of Western Art, completed in 1959, is the work of Le Corbusier and its collection includes works by Renoir, Degas, Tintoretto and Rubens, as well as Miró, Picasso and Jackson Pollock. The courtyard has 57 Rodin sculptures.

Tosho-gu

Just past the Tokyo Metropolitan Art Museum is **Ueno Zoo** (Ueno Dobutsuen; www.tokyo-zoo.net; Tue–Sun 9.30am–5pm), Japan's oldest zoo. South past the entrance is a stone *torii* leading to **Tosho-gu** ⑭ (www.uenotoshogu. com), a shrine completed in 1651 and dedicated to the first shogun, Tokugawa Ieyasu. The approach to the shrine is lined with 200 stone lanterns, while fences on either side of the 'Chinese Gate' have superb carvings of fish, shells, birds and animals attributed to Hidari Jingoro, a bril-

liant Edo-period sculptor. According to legend, two realistic golden dragons which are carved onto the gate would slip off each night to drink from the waters of the nearby Shinobazu Pond.

Saigo Takamori Statue

Follow the paths under the trees past the wooden pillars of the **Kiyomizu Kannon-do**, a temple housing the Thousand-Armed Kannon, and stop for a moment to admire the large bronze statue of **Saigo Takamori** ⑮ on your left. Saigo (1827–73), one of the key architects of the Meiji Restoration, led an unsuccessful rebellion against its new leaders. He eventually committed ritual suicide. The statue shows him dressed in a kimono walking his dog. Slightly northeast of the statue is the restaurant **Oto Oto**, see ❷.

Shinobazu Pond and Benten-do

Take the steps behind Kiyomizu Kannon-do leading down to **Shinobazu Pond** ⑯ (Shinobazu-no-ike). Once an inlet of Tokyo Bay, the pond is now split into three freshwater sections. The first, carpeted with lotus plants and reeds, is a sanctuary for many species of bird and fowl, including black cormorants, egrets, grebes and pintail ducks. The second part of the pond abuts Ueno Zoo, and the third is a small boating lake. A short causeway leads to **Benten-do** ⑰, an octagonal-roofed temple located on a small island. An eight-armed statue of Benzaiten, goddess of the arts, is enshrined here in the main hall.

Penguins in Ueno Zoo *Yanaka Ginza*

Shitamachi Museum

Facing the southeastern corner of the pond is the interesting **Shitamachi Museum** ⑱ (Shitamachi Fuzoku Shiryokan; www.taitocity.net/taito/shitamachi; Tue–Sun 9.30am–4.30pm). Extremely well designed, the museum evokes the huddled world of the common people who lived in the central areas of the city. Exhibits include utensils, tools, toys and furniture. There are also video presentations and photo exhibits, reconstructions of a merchant's house and narrow one-storey homes called *nagaya*. Near the museum you will find the venerable grilled-eel restaurant **Izuei**, see ③.

AMEYA YOKOCHO

When you leave the museum, walk across Chuo-dori to the area slightly south of Ueno Station to find the entrance to the effervescent shopping street and market area called **Ameya Yokocho** ⑲. The name comes from the *ame*, meaning 'sweets', and *yokocho*, the word for 'alley', and it was a black-market zone for many years after World War II. Here, under the railway tracks, among the cheap clothes, fried-noodle vendors and dried-fish stalls, where young men hack blocks of ice and bellow the latest prices for strips of black seaweed, kelp and octopus, the working-class spirit of Shitamachi lives on.

Food and drink

① HANTEI

2-12-15 Nezu, Bunkyo-ku; tel: 3828 1440; Tue–Sat noon–2.30pm and 5–10pm, Sun until 9.30pm; station: Nezu; ¥¥¥
Kushiage (deep-fried skewers of fish, meat and vegetables) are served in a charming wooden building, constructed around a stone storehouse and located in one of Tokyo's best-preserved historic areas.

② OTO OTO

Bamboo Garden, 1-52 Ueno-koen, Taito-ku; tel: 5807 2244; Mon–Fri 11am–3pm and 4.30–11.30pm, Sat 11am–11.30pm, Sun 11am–10pm; station: Ueno; ¥¥

On the middle floor of the Bamboo Garden dining complex, where you will also find Korean and Chinese restaurants, Oto Oto serves a broad range of Japanese favourites, including soba noodles, *donburi* rice bowls and *sashimi* platters.

③ IZUEI

2-12-22 Ueno, Taito-ku; tel: 3831 0954; www.izuei.co.jp; daily 11am–9.30pm; station: Ueno; ¥¥¥
Overlooking Shinobazu Pond, Izuei has been serving succulent *unagi* (grilled-eel) dishes for over 250 years. Sit at a table on the ground floor or on *tatami* mats on the upper levels.

Commuters at Ikebukuro Station

IKEBUKURO & MEJIRODAI

Amble from the tranquil campus of a leafy Ivy League–style university to a classic Japanese garden, via the buzzing commercial heart of Ikebukuro and a cemetery that's the resting place of some of Japan's best-known literary figures.

DISTANCE: 8km (5 miles)
TIME: A leisurely day
START: Ikebukuro Station
END: Edogawabashi Station
POINTS TO NOTE: Do this walk at the weekend and you will be able to see kimono-dressed wedding parties enjoying the gardens at Chinzan-so.

The northwestern suburb of Ikebukuro, meaning 'pond hollow', started out as a marshy wetland of little consequence. The opening of a railway station here in 1903 and, later, the area's first department stores turned the district into a major transport and commercial hub. Today, Ikebukuro is the second-busiest commuter station in Japan after Shinjuku. The area around the station, dominated by big retail, is unexceptional compared to similar Tokyo mini-cities; instead, this route takes you to off-the-beaten-path sights on Ikebukuro's periphery, then south towards a beautiful Japanese garden used as a backdrop for wedding photographs.

WEST IKEBUKURO

Exit on the west side of Ikebukuro Station and head two blocks west to the **Tokyo Metropolitan Theatre ❶** (Tokyo Geijutsu Gekijo; www.geigeki.jp; daily 9am–10pm), a concert, theatre and exhibition venue. Here a giant escalator carries visitors beneath a 28m (90ft) glass atrium up to a hallway with a colourful domed ceiling painted by Koji Kinutani.

Rikkyo University

Cross Gekijo-dori and carry on in a westerly direction through a warren of restaurants and bars, past a small park, until you come to the handsome red-brick gateway to **Rikkyo University ❷**, founded as St Paul's School in 1874 by an American missionary. Its ivy-covered buildings and white-clapboard New England-style faculty houses seem light years away from contemporary Ikebukuro. Stick your head into the main dining room, straight ahead from the entrance, to admire the vaulted wood-beam ceiling.

Tokyo Metropolitan Theatre   *Statues of monks at Gokoku-ji.*

Jiyu Gakuen Myonichikan

Head back to Gekijo-dori, turn right and continue to the junction with the Ikebukuro Police Station. Cross the road and follow the side roads a few blocks south into a residential area to discover **Jiyu Gakuen Myonichikan ❸** (www.jiyu.jp; Tue–Sun 10am–3.30pm), the only Frank Lloyd Wright-designed building still standing in Tokyo. The Myon-ichikan (or 'House of Tomorrow') was originally home to the Jiyu Gakuen school. Appreciate the low-slung building's interior while sipping tea and eating pastries in its central hall. Events such as outdoor cinema screenings and live music concerts are often staged throughout the summer months. Weddings are also held here and at the chapel across the road at weekends.

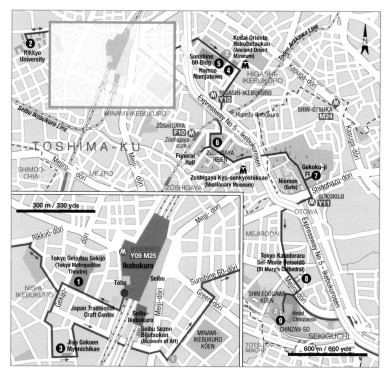

Arcade racing at Namco Namjatown

EAST IKEBUKURO

Returning to the main road, turn right and head for the tunnel beneath the railway tracks, emerging on Meiji-dori. Cross over towards the Junku-do bookstore and walk one block behind it to find **Café Pause**, see ❶.

From here head north to Green-dori, the main boulevard east from the station. Turn left, then right along the mainly pedestrian shopping street Sunshine 60-dori, past several cinemas and a branch of the handicrafts store Tokyu Hands.

Sunshine City

Opposite is the **Sunshine City** complex (www.sunshinecity.jp). Built in 1978, it includes a 60-floor tower, shopping malls, a hotel, theatre, planetarium, aquarium, kids' amusement park and viewing observatory, but looks dated in comparison with contemporary developments such as Tokyo Midtown and Roppongi Hills. However, if you are interested in archaeology and ancient civilisations, visit the **Ancient Orient Museum** ❹ (Kodai Oriento Hakubutsukan; www.aom-tokyo.com; daily 10am–4.30pm) on the seventh floor of Sunshine City's Bunka Kaikan section. Its collection of artefacts from the Indian Subcontinent and the Middle East includes objects excavated by Japanese teams before a dam was built on the Euphrates River.

If you have kids to entertain, or are looking for pop-cultural and culinary curiosities, while you are here stop at **Namco Namjatown** ❺ (www.namja.jp; daily 10am–10pm), an inventively decorated indoor theme park notable for its **Ikebukuro Gyoza Stadium**, see ❷, offering dumplings from chefs around Japan.

Zoshigaya Cemetery

Exit Sunshine City at its southeastern corner and continue south for about five minutes through the side streets towards the raised expressway and Higashi-Ikebukuro subway station, where you will also see the Toden Arakawa tram line. You can hop on the tram here for one stop to Zoshigaya or continue walking for another two minutes to reach **Zoshigaya Cemetery** ❻ (Zoshigaya Reien). This green and tranquil cemetery is the resting place of several well-known figures, including authors Natsume Soseki, Nagai Kafu and Lafcadio Hearn – pick up a map (in Japanese) from the Funeral Hall to locate their graves.

Gokoku-ji

Exit the cemetery at its eastern corner where you will again encounter the raised expressway. Go under, and on the other side you should find an open gate leading into another cemetery in the grounds of **Gokoku-ji** ❼ (www.gokokuji.or.jp). This well-preserved temple complex was established by the fifth shogun, Tokugawa Tsunayoshi, in 1681. The emperor Meiji (1852–1912) is buried here, as are several of his children. Exit the temple by its magnificent gate,

St Mary's Cathedral

Nio-mon, housing two fierce-looking statues placed at either side to ward off evil spirits. If you are tired, the entrance to Gokokuji subway station is also here.

MEJIRODAI

St Mary's Cathedral

Turn right from Gokoku-ji, head back under the expressway, take a left uphill and follow the backstreets south to Mejiro-dori, where you should take a left to arrive at **St Mary's Cathedral** ❽ (daily 9am–5pm) – its tall belltower should guide you. Designed by Kenzo Tange in 1964, the seat of Tokyo's Roman Catholic church, like the architect's Olympic stadium in Yoyogi, still appears strikingly modern. The interior is dominated by a gigantic pipe organ, the largest of its kind in Japan, on which concerts are occasionally given.

Chinzan-So

Opposite the cathedral, a wedding hall and the Hotel Chinzanso share the view across the lovely garden of **Chinzan-so** ❾ (www.hotel-chinzanso-tokyo. jp; daily 9am–8pm). Meaning 'House of Camellia', the garden, designed in the late 19th century, includes a 1,000-year-old pagoda that originally hails from a temple in Hiroshima Prefecture, ancient stone lanterns and monuments, and several restaurants including **Mucha-an**, see ❸. From Chinzan-so, it's around a 10-minute walk downhill back towards the raised expressway to find the entrance to Edogawabashi Station.

Food and drink

❶ CAFÉ PAUSE

2-14-12 Minami-Ikebukuro, Toshima-ku; tel: 6912 7711; www.cafepause.jp; Mon–Thu 11am–9pm, Fri 11am–11pm, Sat and Sun 9am–11pm; station: Ikebukuro; ¥

Contemporary pop culture infuses this laid-back café and gallery, that hosts art exhibitions and events.

❷ IKEBUKURO GYOZA STADIUM

Namco Namjatown, 2F Sunshine City, 3-1 Higashi-Ikebukuro, Toshima-ku; tel: 5950 0765; www.namco.co.jp; daily 10am–10pm; station: Ikebukuro; ¥¥

After fried and boiled dumplings stuffed with prawns, beef, pork, and even kimchee and cheese, go upstairs to Ice Cream City to taste an amazing range of flavours.

❸ MUCHA-AN

Chinzan-so, 2-10-8 Sekiguchi, Bunkyo-ku; tel: 3943 5489; www.chinzanso.com; daily 11.30am–3.30pm and 5–8pm; station: Edogawabashi; ¥¥

Slurp hot or cold soba noodles – the duck (kami) soup ones are delicious – at this small restaurant tucked behind a bamboo grove in Chinzan-so.

ASAKUSA

Experience the lively atmosphere around one of Tokyo's most famous temples on this walk through Asakusa, followed by a short cruise down the Sumida River to a beautiful bayside garden.

DISTANCE: 4km (2.5 miles)
TIME: 6 hours
START/END: Asakusa Station
POINTS TO NOTE: If you take the river cruise at the end of this walk to Hama Rikyu Teien, then the closest subway station is Tsukiji-Shijo, from where you can follow the route to Tsukudajima (see page 76).

This traditional Tokyo district, northeast of the Imperial Palace and centred around the major Buddhist temple Senso-ji, has retained the bustling commerce and ribald good humour that made it the heart of the Edo-era Shitamachi ('low city'). Festivals are constantly celebrated here, and it's a great area for traditional craft and souvenir stores.

SENSO-JI

Enshrining a golden statue of Kannon, goddess of mercy – said to have been fished out of the nearby river in 628AD – Senso-ji is Asakusa's spiritual cen-

tre. The temple's central compound is best approached after passing under the **Kaminari-mon ❶** (Thunder Gate), an impressive wooden entrance flanked by leering twin meteorological deities (Fujin, god of wind, on the right, and Raijin, god of thunder, on the left).

Nakamise-dori

Stretching for about 400m/yds from Kaminari-mon to Senso-ji's main hall of worship is **Nakamise-dori ❷**, a perpetually thronged avenue of colourful stalls selling an amazing variety of products, from the traditional (rice crackers and paper fans) to the bizarre (clothes for dogs).

Either side of Nakamise-dori you will find more of the traditional craft shops that make browsing around Asakusa such a pleasure. Beside Kaminari-mon to the right is **Kurodaya ❸** (Tue–Sun 11am–7pm); in business since 1856, the shop sells traditional woodblock prints and *washi* paper products. Where Nakamise-dori crosses Denboin-dori, turn left to find **Yonoya Kushiho ❹** (Thu–Tue 10.30am–6pm) on the left. The shop is much sought out for its

Kaminari-mon, or Thunder Gate

traditional hairpieces, ornaments and exquisite boxwood combs.

Now head right from Nakamise-dori along Denboin-dori and turn left up Metoro-dori to arrive at **Fujiya ❺** (tel: 3841 2283; Thu–Tue 10am–6pm), specialising in *tenugui* (hand-printed towels with original designs). A little further up, to the right, **Hyakusuke ❻** (Wed–Mon 11am–5pm) is another esoteric shopping experience, having supplied local geisha and *kabuki* actors with cosmetics for more than 100 years.

The central compound

At the head of Nakamise-dori, a second gate, the imposing double-storeyed **Hozo-mon**, disgorges visitors into the wide open grounds that surround the **Senso-ji ❼** (www.senso-ji.jp). Aromatic clouds of incense waft from a large bronze burner that stands here. Visitors immerse themselves and their clothing in this 'breath of the gods' before mounting the broad stone-flagged steps that lead to the temple's main Kannondo hall.

Behind Kannondo, the **Asakusa-jinja ❽** is dedicated to the fishermen brothers who found the Kannon statue back in the 7th century and their lord Haji-no-Nakatomo, who built the original hall to enshrine it in 645. Sadly, this remarkable golden image has remained hidden away in the inner recesses of Senso-ji ever since.

The western half of the Senso-ji compound houses **Gojuno-to**, an impressive 1973 reconstruction of a five-storey pagoda first built at the temple in 942. Its towering vermilion outline stands beside the **Denbo-in ❾**, the residence of Senso-ji's head priest. The building itself is closed to the public, but check to see whether access is permitted to the garden at the small booth just left of the pagoda.

ASAKUSA HANAYASHIKI

West of Senso-ji lies Asakusa's raunchy entertainment district. Adult cinemas, strip clubs, old-fashioned public baths and street barkers are some of the features here. Another local institution is the rickety amusement park **Asakusa Hanayashiki ❿** (www.hanayashiki.net/en; daily 10am–6pm). Dating from 1872, most of the rides and game machines here have a certain vintage quality about them. There's also an eerie *obakiyashiki* (ghost house).

Just west of the amusement park, turn left and follow Rokku Broadway, a shopping

Asakusa's festivals

One of Tokyo's top festivals, the three-day Sanja Matsuri, held on the third weekend in May, sees Asakusa's streets jam-packed as over 100 ornate *mikoshi* (portable shrines) are danced around. It's equally busy in late July when all of Tokyo, dressed in summer *yukata* (cloth robes), descend to watch the spectacular *hanabi* (fireworks) contests held along the Sumida River. As the summer heat reaches its peak at the end of August, Asakusa comes over all Brazilian with a samba carnival.

Azuma Bridge

street that runs parallel to the main Kokus-ai-dori. After you pass the department store ROX, turn right to the main road. Cross over and turn left to reach **Miyamoto Unosuke Shoten ⑪** (www.miyamoto-unosuke.co.jp; Wed–Mon 9am–6pm), a shop with a huge collection of traditional Japanese festival wear and musical instruments. On the store's fourth floor an impressive display of percussion instruments constitutes the **Drum Museum** (Wed–Sun 10am–5pm). Around the corner, to the right, is the popular *okonomiyaki* restaurant **Sometaro**, see ①.

QUIRKY STORES

From Sometaro, keep walking a few blocks west past the rear of the temple Tokyo Hongan-ji to reach Kappabashi-dori, the heart of **Kappabashi ⑫** or Kitchenware Town, a wholesale restaurant equipment area. If you have ever wondered where those life-like plastic food displays in restaurant windows come from, here is your answer.

Return to Kaminarimon-dori and continue to the Sumida River; you can grab a drink nearby at either **Gallery éf**, see ②, or the venerable bar **Kamiya**, see ③. On the other side of the Azuma Bridge (Azuma-bashi) stands one of Tokyo's wackiest pieces of architecture – **Super Dry Hall ⑬** (daily 11.30am–10pm), a beer hall designed by Philippe Starck for the Asahi Beer

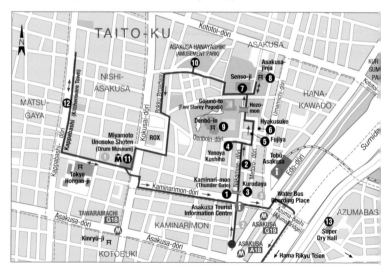

Nakamise-dori   *Tokyo Skytree*

Company and more a sculpture than a building.

TOKYO SKYTREE

Asakusa also makes the best jumping off point for a visit to **Tokyo Skytree** ⓮ (www.tokyo-skytree.jp; 8am–10pm). It's a 15-minute walk across the Sumida or get the train to Tokyo Skytree Station. Tokyo's newest landmark, the satisfyingly conical Skytree is a broadcasting tower that at 634m (2,80ft) is the second-tallest structure in the world. This feat of engineering barely broke a sweat during the severe shaking of Japan's 2011 earthquake; a visit to its observation decks, at 350m (1,148ft) and 450m (1,476ft)

respectively, offers untrammelled views of metropolitan Tokyo out to Mt Fuji and the distant exurbs 70km (43.5 miles) away.

Food and drink

① SOMETARO

2-2-2 Nishi-Asakusa, Taito-ku; tel: 3844 9502; daily noon–10pm; station: Tawaramachi; ¥¥
There are often lines of people waiting outside this rustic eatery, where the speciality is *okonomiyaki*, batter pancakes stuffed with vegetables, shrimp, etc, and covered with lashings of soy sauce and mayonnaise.

② GALLERY ÉF

2-19-18 Kaminari-mon, Taito-ku; tel: 3841 0442; www.gallery-ef.com; Wed–Mon café and gallery 11am–6.30pm, bar 6pm–midnight; station: Asakusa; ¥¥
A trendy café-bar based around a stone-walled *kura* (traditional storehouse), dating from 1868, which is used for art exhibitions. A coffee and cake set menu is ¥750.

③ KAMIYA

1-1-1 Asakusa, Taito-ku; tel: 3841 5400; www.kamiya-bar.com; Wed–Mon 11.30am–10pm; station: Asakusa; ¥¥
In business since 1880, Tokyo's first Western-style bar is famous for its Denkibran ('Electric Brandy') – a stimulating concoction of gin, wine, curaçao and brandy. On the informal ground floor you pay for your food and drinks at the cash desk as you enter, while upstairs it's table service.

View from Eitaibashi Bridge

FUKAGAWA & RYOGOKU

On the eastern side of the Sumida River is little-visited Fukagawa, where you will find a traditional garden, contemporary art galleries and lively temples and shrines, as well as Ryogoku, home to the national sport of sumo wrestling.

DISTANCE: 5km (3 miles)

TIME: A leisurely day

START: Kiyosumi-Shirakawa Station

END: Ryogoku Station

POINTS TO NOTE: The above distance doesn't include the subway ride from Monzen-Nakacho and Ryogoku, which is about 3km (2 miles). Avoid doing this walk on a Monday if you want to visit the art galleries and museums.

Relatively few visitors to Tokyo make it east across the Sumida River, even though the area is steeped in history and has a relaxed old Edo atmosphere and some notable sights. Not only does the district of Fukagawa have interesting temples, shrines and a traditional garden, but it is also making waves on the contemporary art scene as new galleries open up in empty riverside warehouses. North of Fukagawa is Ryogoku, a district primarily associated with sumo wrestling thanks to its being the location of the country's national sumo stadium. It's also where you can find a wonderful museum devoted to the city's history.

FUKAGAWA

Start at the **Fukagawa Edo Museum** ❶ (Fukagawa Edo Shiryokan; 1-3-28 Shirakawa, Koto-ku; www.kcf.or.jp/fukagawa; daily 9.30am–5pm, closed 2nd and 4th Mon of every month), a block directly south of Kiyosumi-Shirakawa Station (take exit A3), where you can experience Fukagawa circa 1842, with evocative displays of homes, shops, a theatre, a boathouse tavern and even a 10m (33ft) fire tower.

The shopping street leading to the museum is charming. It features **Reigan-ji** ❷, a temple dating from 1624, which is best known for its early 18th-century bronze statue of a Jizo figure, seated on a lotus pedestal, and an award-winning public toilet with an Edo-era façade.

Kiyosumi Garden

Return to the crossroads, where Kiyosumi-dori and Kiyosubashi-dori

Kiyosumi Garden

intersect. Cross the road and follow Kiyosubashi-dori to the entrance to the beautiful **Kiyosumi Garden** ❸ (Kiyosumi Teien; http://teien. tokyo-park.or.jp/en/kiyosumi; daily 9am–5pm). This spacious classic *sukiya*-style garden, dating back to the Edo period and designed around a central pond, features an exquisite teahouse that appears to float majestically above the water. Look out for the 55 rare stones gathered from all over Japan by Iwasaki Yataro, the founder of Mitsubishi, who acquired the gardens in the 19th century.

Three bridges

From Kiyosumi head west to the Sumida River, the setting for what is one of the most interesting concentrations of bridges in Japan. A strong nostalgia is attached to these spans, and Tokyoites continue to celebrate them in songs, watercolours, films and novels. First up is the blue-painted **Kiyosu-bashi** ❹, a handsome suspension bridge built in 1928. From here, follow the riverside promenade south to **Sumidagawa-ohashi** ❺; the bridge itself is unattractive due to the flyover above it, but there are great views up- and downstream. Continue for a few minutes until the more graceful blue girders of the 1926 **Eitai-bashi** ❻, one of the oldest bridges on the river, come into view.

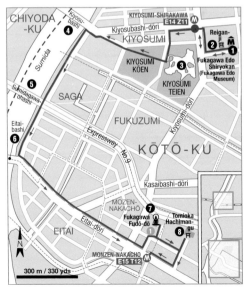

Fukagawa Fudo-do

Staying on this side of the river, walk east along Eitai-dori for about 900m/ yds, until you reach the shopping parade around Monzen-Nakacho Station. Cross Kiyosumi-dori and turn left to find **Fukagawa Fudo-do** ❼, a busy temple of the Shingon sect of Buddhism. The original early 18th-century temple was destroyed in World War II; this one, dating from

Edo–Tokyo Museum

1862, was transported here from Chiba Prefecture outside of Tokyo. The narrow shopping street leading to the temple from exit 1 of Monzen-Nakacho Station is lined with small restaurants and stalls selling *senbei* rice crackers. Try **Kintame**, see ❶, opposite the temple.

Tomioka Hachiman-gu

Just east of the temple is the **Tomioka Hachiman-gu** ❽, a shrine that is the focus of one of Tokyo's greatest festivals, the mid-August Fukagawa Matsuri. A 1968 reconstruction of the 17th-century original, the current shrine has impressive prayer and spirit halls and a towering green copper-tiled roof. It is dedicated to eight deities, including Benten, goddess of beauty and the arts.

The shrine is strongly associated with sumo wrestling and in the Edo era was the official venue for the sport. Walk to the back of the shrine and you will see the **Yokozuna Monument**, engraved with the names of long-departed sumo wrestlers who reached the rank of *ozeki*, the highest in the sumo world.

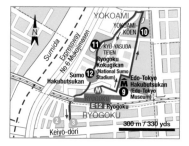

Exit through the shrine's main *torii* gate, and turn right to reach the subway at Monzen-Nakacho. Take the Oedo line three stops north to Ryogoku.

RYOGOKU

Edo-Tokyo Museum

Behind the station exit is the impressive **Edo-Tokyo Museum** ❾ (Edo-Tokyo Hakubutsukan; 1-4-1 Yokoami, Sumida-ku; www.edo-tokyo-museum.or.jp; Tue–Fri and Sun 9.30am–5.30pm, Sat 9.30am–7.30pm), based in a wedge-shaped monolith balanced on four massive pillars. Highlights of the museum, which traces the history of the city from its founding through to the post-war reconstruction years, are replicas of the Nihonbashi, the wooden bridge which stood at the centre of Edo, the residence of a *daimyo* (feudal lord) and a *kabuki stage*. The museum also has well-curated revolving exhibitions of artefacts that can range from giant Edo Era scrolls to a look inside the castles of the Tokugawa Shogunate.

Yokoami Park

One block north of the museum is small **Yokoami Park** ❿ (Yokoami-koen), in which the austere temple-like complex of **Tokyo Ireido** is dedicated to the 100,000 victims of the Great Kanto Earthquake which struck just before noon on 1 September 1923 and destroyed over 70 percent of

Wrestlers at Kokugikan

Tokyo. A small **museum** (Tue–Sun 9am–4.30pm) displays remains from the fateful day.

Kyu-Yasuda Garden

Leave the park by the west gate behind Tokyo Ireido and cross diagonally to reach the small but distinguished **Kyu-Yasuda Garden** ⑪ (Kyu-Yasuda Teien; daily 9am–4.30pm, Jun–Aug until 6pm). Preserving the spirit of an old Edo-period stroll garden, the grounds were acquired in the 1850s by wealthy industrialist and banker Yasuda Zenjiro, grandfather of the avant-garde artist and musician Yoko Ono.

Ryogoku Kokugikan

Immediately south of the garden is the national sumo stadium, **Ryogoku Kokugikan** ⑫ (www.sumo.or.jp/en). Two-week stints of this highly ritualised, visually spectacular sport are held here in January, May and September. There is a small Sumo Museum (Sumo Hakubut-sukan; Mon–Fri 10am–4.30pm) on the same premises.

One of the ways in which sumo wrestlers acquire such giant girths is by consuming bowls of a nutritious, but body-enriching, stew called *chanko-nabe*. If you would like to sample the dish yourself, several restaurants in the area specialise in it. One of the best is **Chanko Kawasaki**, see ②, housed in an atmospheric 1937 building; another is **Tomoegata**, see ③.

Food and drink

① KINTAME

1-14-3 Tomioka, Koto-ku; tel: 3641 4561; www.kintame.co.jp; Tue–Sun 10am–6pm; station: Monzen-Nakacho; ¥¥
Opposite the Fukagawa Fudo-do temple, this appealing place serves tasty Kyoto-style fish marinated in sake lees (deposits produced during fermentation), and a variety of pickles.

② CHANKO KAWASAKI

2-13-1 Ryogoku, Sumida-ku; tel: 3631 2529; Mon–Sat 5–9pm; station: Ryogoku; ¥¥
Like many others in the area, this restaurant specialises in the preferred dish of sumo wrestlers, *chanko-nabe* stews, but it has the edge because of its location in a charming wooden house and its friendly owners. A set meal starts at ¥3,050, and bookings are advised.

③ TOMOEGATA

2-17-6 Ryogoku, Sumida-ku; tel: 3632 5600; www.tomoegata.com; daily 11.30am–2pm and 5–11pm; station: Ryogoku; ¥¥
Fluttering colourful banners mark this restaurant, with branches either side of the road, where you can sample *chanko-nabe*. If you are not so hungry, then the ¥860 *sebisu-chanko* (only served for lunch Monday to Friday) will suffice.

Freshly caught octopus

TSUKUDAJIMA AND TOYOSU

Pay a visit to charming Tsukudajima, a tiny enclave that evokes the Tokyo of centuries ago, tour the legendary Tokyo Metropolitan Central Wholesale Market and top it off with fresh sushi.

DISTANCE: 5km (3 miles)
TIME: A half day
START: Tsukishima Station
END: Toyosu Station
POINTS TO NOTE: October 2018 saw the long-rumoured and controversial relocation of the legendary Tsukiji Fish Market (aka the Tokyo Metropolitan Central Wholesale Market) to its new home in Toyosu. Check the website before visiting to make sure it's open – there are often holidays in addition to the regular Sunday closing. Also note that the fish market has become so popular that rules for visitors have been introduced; now tourists can only experience the famous tuna auctions from a glass-fronted viewing deck. Water-resistant, rubber-soled footwear is recommended for walking through the market. Toyosu is also the terminus for the futuristic Yurikamome monorail through Odaiba should you wish to visit that area in addition.

TSUKUDAJIMA

Meaning 'Island of Cultivated Rice Fields', the name Tsukudajima is a reference to the rural outskirts of Osaka, from where its first settlers came in the 17th century to work primarily as fishermen, supplying the shogun's kitchens with fish, but also as watchmen, keeping an eye on movements in Edo's bay.

By the early Meiji period, Tsukudajima had been combined with the reclaimed islands of Ishikawajima to the north and Tsukishima to the south in one contiguous landfill. Spared the great fires of Edo and the earthquake that struck Tokyo in 1923, the island's huddles of housing blocks, narrow alleyways full of potted plants and old-fashioned street-corner lift-pumps (some still in use) lend Tsukudajima its distinctive character. Many of the houses have traditionally crafted features, including black ceramic roofs, oxidised copper finials of an ancient green patina and well-seasoned wooden walls.

Panorama of Toyosu

Tsukudako Bridge

Exit Tsukishima Station and head north to **Tsukudako Bridge** ❶ (Tsukudako-bashi), an attractive bridge with a red handrail that spans a narrow tidal inlet where you can get a modest insight into the former life of this quarter. The fishermen's shacks and boathouses are less charmingly dilapidated than they were just a few years ago, and the number of their vessels is depleted. Nearby is the ramen restaurant **Tsukishima Rock** see ❶.

Sumiyoshi-jinja

In days of old, visitors to the island brought offerings of *tsukudani* to the **Sumiyoshi-jinja shrine** ❷, less than a minute's walk away to the right and then to the left. Vestiges of the shrine's role as a protector of sea travellers, fishermen and sailors can be seen in carvings on beams and transoms covering some of the small outer buildings. One particularly realistic relief on the roof of the well beside the shrine's *torii* shows fisher-

men in a skiff, with firewood burning in a metal basket as they cast their nets into the bay at night. Continue north to find **Tenyasu Honten** ❸ (daily 9am–6pm), a charming shop selling one of the island's best-known products – *tsukudani* (seaweed and fish preserved in a preparation of salt, soy sauce and sugar). A sampler box of six types of *tsukudani*, which tastes great with rice, costs ¥2,000.

Return to Tsukishima Station and take the subway three stops to Shijo-mae Station.

TOYOSU MARKET

Another rapidly developing bayside area built on landfill, Toyosu is the location of the new **Toyosu Market** ❹ (Tokyo Chuo Oroshiurishijo; www.shijou.metro.tokyo.jp/english/toyosu; Mon–Sat 5am–5pm, check website for occasional holidays). The fish market at Tsukiji was an iconic Tokyo landmark which moved from its former location in October 2018

At the tuna auction

Sumiyoshi Taisha shrine

(see Points to note) to its new home in Toyosu, after 80 years in its Tsukiji home.

It was originally constructed in 1935 after the Great Kantō earthquake dev-

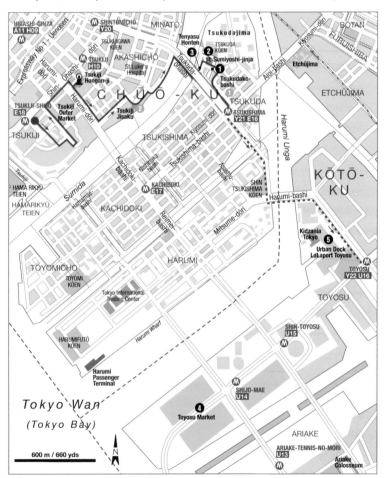

Tsukudako Bridge

astated much of central Tokyo, including the Nihonbashi fish market.

This latest move has proved controversial after the detection of toxic chemicals on the new site prompted an expensive clean-up and delay to the target date. After repeated delays, the new market opened for business in late 2018 in expanded modern facilities.

Wholesalers start laying out their stalls and preparing for the 5.30am tuna auction in the dead of night. The best cuts of these rock-hard fish, lined up like frozen sputniks and marked in red paint with their country of origin and weight, sell wholesale for as much as ¥10,000 per kilo, several times the price of the most expensive prime beef. Sadly viewing the tuna auction as a tourist is no longer the vivid, up-close experience it was at Tsukiji, with the public now limited to watching proceedings from behind glass on an observation deck. Limited tickets are available on a lottery basis for a closer viewing deck on the lower floor; you can apply at www.shijou.metro.tokyo.jp/english/toyosu. At 7am the fruit and vegetable auctions start, and the action keeps buzzing as vendors hawk some 450 different types of fish. Things begin to tail off in the fish market around 8am, although the market itself and many of its shops and restaurants stay open until 5pm. Whenever you visit, top off your tour with a scrumptious meal of fresh sushi at one of the many seafood specialists located in the outer market.

URBAN DOCK LALAPORT TOYOSU

Should you have time, Toyosu is also home to the 21st-century retail experience that is **Urban Dock LaLaport Toyosu ⑤** (http://toyosu.lalaport.jp; daily 10am–11pm). Alongside the shops, restaurants and multiplex cinema here, you will find **Ukiyo-e Tokyo** (Tue–Fri noon–7pm, Sat–Sun 11am–7pm), a small exhibition of traditional woodblock prints, and **Kidzania Tokyo** (www.kidzania.jp; daily 9am–3pm, 4–9pm), an indoor theme park..

Stop at Tsukiji Jisaku, see ②, for dinner on the way back to the station.

Food and drink

① TSUKISHIMA ROCK

2-16-7 Tsukuda, Chuo-ku; tel: 3532 3172; daily 11.30am–2.30pm and 6pm–midnight; station: Tskukishima; ¥
Generous bowls of hearty ramen are the order of the day at this stylish restaurant, accompanied by a rock 'n' roll soundtrack and lengthy sake menu.

② TSUKIJI JISAKU

14-19 Akashicho, Chuo-ku; tel: 3541 2391; www.jisaku.co.jp; Mon–Fri 5–10pm, Sat 11am–10pm, Sun 11am–6pm; station: Tsukiji; ¥¥¥¥
If you have guests to impress, come to this elegant, traditional mansion with manicured-garden views and waitresses in kimonos serving *kaiseki ryori* – Japanese haute cuisine.

The Giant Sky Wheel at Palette Town

ODAIBA

Ride the monorail out into Tokyo Bay to explore this man-made island of futuristic buildings, interesting museums and quirky shopping malls. Finish with a bath at a hot-spring complex and a walk across the Rainbow Bridge.

> **DISTANCE:** 7.5km (4.75 miles)
> **TIME:** A half day
> **START:** Kokusai-Tenjijo-Seimon Station/Tokyo Big Sight
> **END:** Shibaura-Futo Station
> **POINTS TO NOTE:** A ¥820 one-day ticket for the Yurikamome monorail (www.yurikamome.tokyo), connecting with Tokyo's subway at Shimbashi and Toyosu stations, lets you hop on and off at will.

TOKYO BIG SIGHT

Heading by monorail to the east of the island of Odaiba, you can't fail to miss the gravity-defying **Tokyo Big Sight ❶** (www.bigsight.jp), a massive convention centre. It consists of four inverted pyramids and is best accessed from Kokusai-Tenjijo-Seimon monorail station, outside of which there's a sculpture depicting a huge upended saw.

Follow the monorail tracks southwest in the direction of a highly visible Ferris wheel – the **Giant Sky Wheel** (charge). The wheel is part of **Palette Town ❷**,

a colourful recreational complex that includes the quirky pseudo-neoclassical **Venus Fort** (www.venusfort.co.jp) mall, with a ceiling illuminated by an electronic sky that changes by the minute.

AROUND MIRAIKAN

Walk south then west past the blue arch of the Telecom Centre to the **National Museum of Emerging Science and Innovation ❸** (www.miraikan.jst.go.jp; Wed–Mon 10am–5pm), also known as the **Miraikan**, where you can learn about robot technology and other cutting-edge science projects.

> ## Food and drink
>
> **❶ KHAZANA**
> 5F Decks Tokyo Beach, 1-6-1 Daiba, Minato-ku; tel: 3599 6551; www.maharaja-group.com; daily 11am–11pm; station: Odaiba-Kaihin-koen; ¥¥
> Khazana offers all-you-can-eat Indian lunches (until 5pm) and good curries, plus outside tables with views of the Rainbow Bridge.

Oedo Onsen Monogatari

Nearby soothe your limbs at the extraordinary **Oedo Onsen Monogatari** ❹ (www.ooedoonsen.jp; daily 11am–9am (last entry 7am)) a traditional hot-spring bath with outdoor and indoor tubs, a sand bath, saunas and foot-massage baths.

A short walk northwest of the Miraikan is the **Museum of Maritime Science** ❺ (Fune-no-Kagakukan; www.funenok agakukan.or.jp; Tue–Sun 10am–5pm). The building has exhibitions tracing the development of shipping and sea transport. Docked outside and part of the museum are the decommissioned ferry *Yoteimaru* and *The Soya*, used for Japanese expeditions to the Antarctic.

DIVERCITY TOKYO PLAZA

Heading north through the West Promenade, you will see **DiverCity Tokyo**

Plaza ❻ (1-1-10 Aomi, Koto-ku; www. divercity-tokyo.com; daily 10am–11pm), another vast shopping and recreational complex. The most notable attraction here is **Round 1 Stadium** (DiverCity Tokyo Plaza 6F; www.round1.co.jp/shop/tenpo/tokyo-divercity.html; Mon–Thu 8am–6am, Fri 8am–Mon 6am). Recommended for those with kids, visitors can enjoy bowling, karaoke and pool.

ODAIBA BEACH

Walk to the northern edge of the island, where you will find an artificial **beach** and Daiba Station, to view the astonishing Kenzo Tange-designed **Fuji TV Building** ❼.

From the next monorail station – Odaiba-Kaihin-koen – you can access **Decks Tokyo Beach** ❽ (www.odai ba-decks.com), a shopping and amusement complex that includes the state-of-art arcade **Joypolis** (daily 10am–10pm) and plenty of places to eat, including **Khazana**, see ❶.

RAINBOW BRIDGE

From Odaiba-Kaihin-koen Station a walkway leads up across the 918m (3,000ft) long **Rainbow Bridge** ❾. A pedestrian promenade links the two anchorages at each end of the suspension bridge.

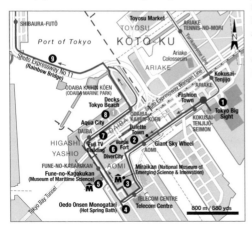

Kurazukuri rooftops

KAWAGOE

Less than an hour north of Tokyo, discover this 'Little Edo', famed for its historic core of kurazukuri – black-walled merchant houses, some dating from the 18th century – and the transported remains of Edo Castle.

DISTANCE: 40km (25 miles) north from Tokyo to Kawagoe; walking tour: 8km (5 miles)
TIME: A full day
START/END: Kawagoe Station
POINTS TO NOTE: Kawagoe is served by three train lines: JR, Seibu-Shinjuku and Tobu. The Tobu line express from Ikebukuro in Tokyo offers the fastest journey (30 min; ¥450), but the JR service only takes a few minutes longer and passes through Kawagoe Station, the start of this walk. Seibu-Shinjuku line trains (43 min from Shinjuku; ¥480) terminate at Hon-Kawagoe Station, about 1km (0.6 mile) closer to Kawagoe's historic core. Avoid Mondays, when several of the museums are closed.

Affectionately known as 'Little Edo', the old castle town of Kawagoe is a favourite of television directors looking for a ready-made set for historical dramas. The rivers that surround Kawagoe made it a strategic location on the way to the capital, and the town prospered as a supplier of goods to Edo (Tokyo) during the Tokugawa era (1603–1867). Now part of the Greater Tokyo area and a commuter suburb, it provides a glimpse of what most of the capital looked like before World War II and relentless modernisation both took their toll.

There's a tourist information office (www.koedo.or.jp; daily 9am–4.30pm) at Kawagoe Station, where you can pick up a map of the town and an English pamphlet on the sights.

KUMANO-JINJA

From Kawagoe Station, it's a 15-minute walk to the town's historic core around Ichiban-gai. Follow the walkway on the left in front of the station to the Atre Department Store, walk down the steps and across the traffic lights to the Crea Mall, a busy pedestrian shopping street leading towards Ichiban-gai. At the first major intersection after about a 0.5km (0.3 mile), head one street to the left to reach Chuo-dori. On the right you will pass **Kumano-jinja ❶**, a small shrine housing one of the floats (called *dashi*) used in Kawagoe's lively annual festival.

Competitors march during the Kawagoe Festival

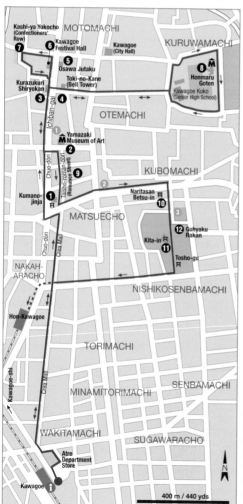

AROUND ICHIBAN-GAI

A couple of short blocks later, you will know you have reached Ichiban-gai when you see the first *kurazukuri*, to the right. This impressive merchant building used to house the Kameya sweet shop and factory, and is now the **Yamazaki Museum of Art** ❷ (Fri–Wed 9.30am–5pm), displaying screen paintings by the 19th-century artist Gaho Hashimoto. Entry includes a cup of tea and a traditional Japanese sweet *(okashi)*. Around the corner on Ichiban-gai is a functioning sweet shop and café, **Kurazukuri Honpo**, see ❶.

As well as confectionery shops, Ichiban-gai is lined with other interesting stores, including ones that specialise in ceramics, knives, swords and woodwork items. Inside an old tobacco wholesaler you will find the **Kurazukuri Shiryokan** ❸ (Tue–Sun 9am–4.30pm). This is one of the first *kurazukuri* to

be rebuilt after the great fire of 1893 that wiped out over a third of the city.

Across the road from the Kurazukuri Shiryokan down a lane to the right is the **Toki-no-Kane** ❹, a three-storey wooden belltower that has become synonymous with Kawagoe. The tower was originally constructed in the 17th century and has since been through four editions, the most recent being this one dating from after the 1893 fire. Listen out for the bell, which tolls four times daily – at 6am, noon, 3pm and 6pm.

Further along the Ichiban-gai is the **Osawa Jutaku** ❺. Dating from 1792, it is Kawagoe's oldest kurazukuri and now a handicraft shop that sells traditional products like Japanese masks and dolls.

Opposite is the **Kawagoe Festival Hall** ❻ (daily Apr–Sept 9.30am–6pm,

Oct–Mar 9.30am–5pm, closed 2nd and 4th Wed of the month), in which you can view two more of the ornate floats paraded around in the Kawagoe Festival, along with videos of past events.

At the next main intersection after the Kawagoe Festival Hall turn left and walk a block to reach the narrow stone-paved lane on the left that is **Kashi-ya Yokocho** ❼, 'Confectioners' Row'. Souvenirs and trinkets have been added to the 22 nostalgically old-fashioned shops that sell traditional candies, crackers and other sweet treats such as purple sweet potato ice cream.

REMAINS OF KAWAGOE CASTLE

Return to the belltower and walk east until you come to a school at the end of the street. You will need to loop round the school to find the one-time location of Kawagoe Castle. All that remains of the original fort is the entrance and main visitors' hall of the palace building, **Honmaru Goten** ❽ (Tue–Sun 9am–5pm). Built by a local lord, Matsudaira Naritsune, in 1848, it's now a museum containing beautifully painted screens and waxwork dummies of samurai and lords of old.

TAISHO ROMANCE STREET

Retrace your route from Honmaru Goten back to the Yamazaki Art Museum. Running parallel to Chuo-dori one block to the east is **Taisho-roman-dori** ❾, meaning Taisho Romance Street. The handsome stone

Kawagoe Festival

Considered to be one of the Kanto area's top three festivals, Kawagoe's grand *matsuri*, held on the third Saturday and Sunday of October, attracts huge crowds. The tradition, which started back in the late 17th century, now sees some 25 extravagantly decorated floats, each representing a different area of the city and attended by costumed teams, parade through the streets around Ichiban-gai. The highlight of the festival is the Hikkawase – the Pulling of the Floats – when passing teams square off against each other in a cacophonous performance of music and chanting.

Statues at Gohyaku Rakan

façades of the shops here date from the Taisho era (1912–26) and contrast nicely with those of the nearby *kurazukuri*. Before the street leads back into the Crea Mall turn left and walk east for one block to find the grilled-eel restaurant **Ichinoya**, see ②.

A short walk east of Ichinoya is the temple **Naritasan Betsu-in** ⑩ . On the 28th of each month, a flea market is hosted in its grounds.

KITA-IN

Immediately after the temple turn right and head a few blocks south, past the noodle restaurant **Kotobukian**, see ③, to reach **Kita-in** ⑪ (www.kawagoe.com/kitain; Mar–Dec Mon–Sat 8.50am–4.30pm, Sun until 4.50pm, Dec–Feb Mon–Sat 8.50am–4pm, sun until 4.20pm), an important Buddhist temple-museum that dates back to 830. It has been destroyed several times by fire, but after one conflagration in 1638, the third shogun, Tokugawa Iemitsu, ordered that parts of the original Edo Castle (situated where the Imperial Palace now stands) be transported here to aid in the reconstruction. From these historic wooden buildings you can admire a traditional Japanese garden planted with plum, cherry and maple trees as well as hydrangea and azaleas.

Gohyaku Rakan

Apart from the Edo Castle remains, Kita-in's other crowd-pleaser is the **Gohyaku Rakan** ⑫ grove of stone stat-ues carved between 1782 and 1825. Meaning '500 statues', there are actually 540 depictions of the disciples of the Buddha, no two alike.

While at the temple you can also admire a mini-version of Nikko's **Tosho-gu**, built to honour Tokugawa Ieyasu, the first shogun.

Exit the temple to the south, turn right and walk around 1km (0.6 mile) back towards Crea Mall and either the Hon-Kawagoe or Kawagoe Station to return to Tokyo.

Food and drink

① KURAZUKURI HONPO

Ichiban-gai; daily 10am–5pm; ¥
Kawagoe is famous for edible creations made from *satsaimo* (sweet potato). You can try some at this confectionery shop and café.

② ICHINOYA

1-18-10 Matsue-cho; tel: 049-222 0354; www.unagi-ichinoya.jp; daily 11am–8.30pm; ¥¥
The delicacy *unagi* (grilled eel) is served at this popular two-floor restaurant. Sit on *tatami* mats and enjoy a set lunch of the savoury-sweet fish with rice.

③ KOTOBUKIAN

1-2-11 Kosemba-cho; tel: 049-225 1184; Mon–Tue and Thu–Fri 11.30am–5pm; ¥¥
Located beside Kita-in, this restaurant specialises in *wariko-soba* – green-tea buckwheat noodles served in lacquered bento boxes with a variety of other dishes.

The Tsurugaoka shrine

KAMAKURA & ENOSHIMA

Spend the day at the seaside discovering the venerable Zen temples and shrines of Japan's ancient capital, Kamakura. Come face to face with the Daibutsu (Great Buddha), then visit the sacred island of Enoshima.

DISTANCE: 45km (28 miles) from Toyko to Kamakura
TOUR: 11.5km (7.25 miles)
TIME: A full day
START: Kita-Kamakura Station
END: Enoshima Station
POINTS TO NOTE: Either take a JR Yokosuka line train from Tokyo Station or a JR Shonan-Shinjuku line train from Shinjuku or Shibuya. Make sure the train is bound for Yokosuka or Kurihama, otherwise you will have to change at Ofuna. It's worth investing in the Kamakura Enoshima Pass (www.jreast. co.jp/e/pass/kamakura_enoshima. html; ¥700), a one-day discount ticket covering local JR trains from Ofuna and Enoshima stations, the jumping off points for trains from Tokyo, plus unlimited travel on the Enoden line (www. enoden.co.jp) and Shonan monorail connecting Enoshima with Ofuna.

Wedged between wooded hills and the sea, just one hour south by train from central Tokyo, Kamakura is saturated in history.

With a proliferation of temples and shrines, the town served between 1192 and 1333 as the shogun's capital. If you are only visiting for the day, it's best to stick to a few carefully selected highlights and leave some time to enjoy the beaches and ocean vistas around neighbouring Enoshima.

At Kamakura Station there is a tourist information office (daily 9am–5pm) where the staff speak English. Free maps are available, and they can tell you where to rent a bike should you wish to pedal around the area.

KAMAKURA

A cluster of temples just five minutes' walk from Kita-Kamakura Station is the ideal place to begin. Surrounded by ancient cedars, **Engaku-ji ❶** (daily Apr–Oct 8am–5pm, Nov–Mar 8am–4pm), a major Zen temple founded in 1282 to honour soldiers killed during Kublai Khan's failed invasion of the country, is the closest. Laid out according to Chinese Zen principles, the main buildings and numerous sub-temples evoke an austere beauty, softened by foliage, shrubbery

Tranquil Engaku-ji *Lighting the incense burner*

and a pond. The Chinese-style Shari-den, one of the finest buildings here, is said to contain a tooth of the Buddha.

Tokei-ji

Continue southeast along the main road until you reach **Tokei-ji ❷** (www.tokeiji.com; daily Mar–Oct 8.30am–5pm, Nov–Feb 8.30am–4pm), a 13th-century Buddhist temple that originally served as a nunnery. Also known as the 'Divorce Temple', this was one of the few places where women could escape from abusive husbands. Stroll through the flower-filled gardens to the temple's rear where, in a modest cemetery, lie the remains of the nuns. On leaving, you will pass the vegetarian restaurant **Hachi-no-ki**, see ❶, on the main road.

Kencho-ji

Follow the main Kamakura-kaido road across the railway tracks until you reach

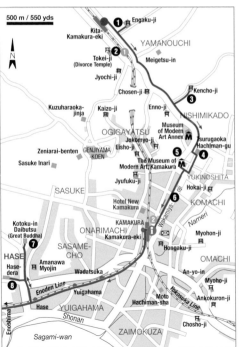

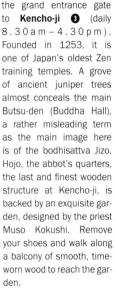

the grand entrance gate to **Kencho-ji ❸** (daily 8.30am–4.30pm). Founded in 1253, it is one of Japan's oldest Zen training temples. A grove of ancient juniper trees almost conceals the main Butsu-den (Buddha Hall), a rather misleading term as the main image here is of the bodhisattva Jizo. Hojo, the abbot's quarters, the last and finest wooden structure at Kencho-ji, is backed by an exquisite garden, designed by the priest Muso Kokushi. Remove your shoes and walk along a balcony of smooth, time-worn wood to reach the garden.

Tsuruoaka Hachiman-gu

Continue downhill towards the centre of

Visiting the Great Buddha

Kamakura until you reach the rear entrance to the shrine **Tsurugaoka Hachiman-gu** ④, marked by a series of red-painted *torii* (entrance gates). Since the 11th century this has been the guardian shrine for the Minamoto clan, founders of the Kamakura shogunate. Most of the buildings are reconstructions, but the red-painted halls, souvenir stalls and flow of visitors make it one of the city's most colourful pilgrimage spots.

Within the shrine precincts you will also find the **Museum of Modern Art, Kamakura** ⑤ (www.moma.pref.kanagawa.jp/en; Tue–Sun 9.30am–5pm), which has regular exhibitions of Japanese and foreign artists. The museum's annex is back on the main road before Tsurugaoka Hachiman-gu. It has recently undergone significant renovations and is due to reopen in September 2019.

Cross the Drum Bridge and exit the shrine onto **Wakamiya-oji** ⑥. This boulevard, with its central reservation

planted with cherry trees and azaleas, is a popular flower-viewing site in spring. Walk until you reach the mock *torii* gate at the end of the central reservation, and turn right to find **Nakamura-an**, see ② , one of Kamakura's most famous noodle restaurants. From here it is less than a minute's walk west to Kamakura Station.

HASE

To reach the next sight, you will need to use the Enoden line train which connects Kamakura and Enoshima. Board the train at Kamakura Station and alight three stops later at **Hase**. From here it's just a few minutes' walk north along the main street to the entrance of **Kotoku-in** ⑦ (daily Apr–Sept 8am–5.30pm, Oct–Mar 8am–5pm), which houses the *Daibutsu* – the Great Buddha. This 11m (35ft) image of Amida Nyorai, the Buddha who receives souls into the Western Paradise, is Japan's second-largest

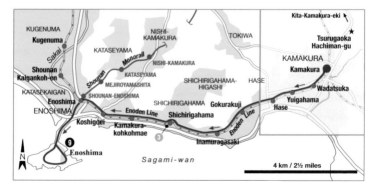

A view of Mount Fuji and Enoshima

bronze statue. Cast in 1252, it was originally housed in a wooden hall that suffered a series of catastrophes, culminating in a great tidal wave that swept the building away in 1495. These disasters were interpreted as a sign that the Buddha wished to remain outside.

Return in the direction of Hase Station, turn right and enter the grounds of the 8th-century temple **Hase-dera** ❽ (www.hasedera.jp; daily Mar–Sept 8am–5pm, Oct–Feb 8am–4.30pm). Walk past an ornamental pond and up a flight of steps to reach the main temple precincts, which have fine views of Kamakura Bay. The temple is renowned for its eleven-faced Kannon, made from a single camphor and covered in gold leaf.

ENOSHIMA

Board the Enoden train again and get off at Enoshima Station. It's a 15-minute walk from here and across the 600m/yd causeway to the tiny sacred island of **Enoshima** ❾, its hilly slopes plastered with an extraordinary collection of shrines, grottoes and souvenir shops. Local fishermen traditionally came to Enoshima to pray for a bountiful catch. Escalators take the faithful to higher reaches, but it's not difficult to follow the old pilgrim routes as they wind up through this island of the gods.

If you would like to enjoy a meal or cocktail before leaving the seaside, though, a recommended spot to do so is the less touristy restaurant and bar

Bills, see ❸, steps away from Shichi-rigahama Station on the Enoden line, a few stops back towards Kamakura.

Food and drink

❶ HACHI-NO-KI

7 Yamanouchi, Kamakura; tel: 0467-23 3723; www.hachinoki.co.jp; Tue–Fri 11.30am–2.30pm, 5–9pm, Sat–Sun 11am–3pm, 5–9pm; ¥¥

Next to Kencho-ji, this is the main branch of a famous restaurant serving the delicate Buddhist vegetarian cuisine known as *shojin ryori*. If it's full, there's another branch closer to Kita-Kamakura Station.

❷ NAKAMURA-AN

1-7-6 Komachi, Kamakura; tel: 0467-253 500; www.nakamura-an.com; daily 11.15am–5pm; ¥

There's almost always a queue in this rustic *soba* restaurant, where the buckwheat noodles are handmade and cheap.

❸ BILLS

Weekend House Alley 2F, 1-1-1 Shichirigahama, Kamakura; tel: 0467-392 244; https://billsjapan.com/en/shichirigahama; Mon 7am–5pm, Tue–Sun 7am–9pm; ¥¥

Sydney-based chef Bill Granger brings his famous scrambled eggs and laid-back brand of cuisine to this sunny, sophisticated spot overlooking Shichirigahama Beach.

A Hakone Tozan Railway train

HAKONE

This excursion, covering the hot-spring and lakeside resort of Hakone, takes in a range of museums, historical sights, Japan's oldest European-style hotel and – if the weather plays ball – postcard views of Mount Fuji.

DISTANCE: 90km (56 miles) southwest from Tokyo to Hakone; tour: 26km (16 miles)

TIME: 1 or 2 days

START/END: Hakone-Yumoto Station

POINTS TO NOTE: At a brisk clip, you can cover this itinerary in a day. Whether you do this or spend a couple of days here, save money with the Hakone Free Pass (¥6,100 for three days, ¥5,700 for two days), both of which cover a return trip on the Odakyu line from Shinjuku to Odawara, plus unlimited use of the Hakone Tozan Railway, Sounzan funicular, Hakone Ropeway, boats on Lake Ashino and most local buses. They also get you discounts at many of Hakone's attractions. For ¥1,190, ride the Odakyu line's 'Romancecar', a direct express train from Shinjuku Station to Hakone-Yumoto. For more details, see www.odakyu.jp. If possible, visit Hakone on a weekday, when it is quieter.

Stressed out Tokyoites flock to Hakone to relax in the local *onsen* – hot-spring baths

– and enjoy the scenic surroundings. Join the fun of touring the region on multiple forms of transport, including a cable car across a steaming volcanic field and a mock-17th-century galleon over a lovely lake with Mount Fuji in the background.

HAKONE-YUMOTO

The circular route begins at **Hakone-Yumoto ❶**, a tourist town jam-packed with souvenir shops and resort hotels. Its saving grace is its excellent *onsen*, the most convenient of which is the small **Kappa Tengoku Notemburo** (777 Yumoto; tel: 0460-856 121; daily 10am–10pm), a short walk uphill from the train station, offering outdoor baths (called *rotemburo*).

HAKONE TOZAN RAILWAY

Connect to the **Hakone Tozan Railway ❷** at Hakone-Yumoto Station. The line, which has the feeling of a delightfully slow trolley car, has several switchbacks to cope with the mountain slopes. As the train negotiates the inclines, the carriages virtually brush the camellias, azaleas, hydrangeas

One of Hakone-Yumoto's outdoor baths

and other flowering shrubs and bushes that grow beside the track or on the borders of dense wooded areas along the way.

FUJIYA HOTEL

Alight at Miyanoshita Station. This village and hot-spring resort is located along a ravine; it is just a short walk from the station to the historic **Fujiya Hotel** ❸ (tel: 0460-822 211; www.fujiyahotel.jp/en), dating from 1878 when it was Japan's first European-style hotel. With its 1930s wood-panelled dining room, a library full of old books, and waitresses in Agatha Christie-period uniforms, it remains a charming place, set to be even more attractive once it reopens in April 2020 after renovations. Whether or not you stay, it's worth eating at the **Kika-so-Inn**, see ❶.

HAKONE OPEN-AIR MUSEUM

Return to the Tozan line and continue for another two stops until you arrive at Chokoku-no-Mori, the station for the **Hakone Open-Air Museum** ❹ (tel: 0460-821 161; www.hakone-oam. or.jp; daily 9am–5pm). It features modern sculptures by the likes of Calder, Brancusi, Rodin, Giacometti, Henry Moore and other Western masters, artfully placed in landscaped gardens that afford superb views of sea and mountains. The Picasso Pavilion contains sculptures, paintings, ceramics and tiles, as well as galleries devoted to Renoir, Chagall, Miró and Japanese artists, such as Hayashi Takeshi and Umehara Ryuzaburo. There are several

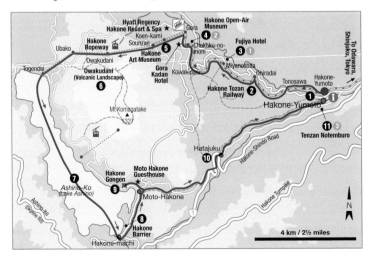

In the tourist town of Hakone–Yumoto

places to eat at the museum, including the restaurant **Bella Foresta**, see ②.

HAKONE ART MUSEUM

The terminus of the Tozan line is only one stop away from the museum at **Gora**. Here, transfer to a **funicular tram** for the 10-minute journey to Sounzan, the starting point for the cable car that crosses Mount Soun.

Before that, though, get off at Koen-kami Station on the funicular to visit the **Hakone Art Museum** ❺ (Fri–Wed 9.30am–4.30pm), which specialises in Japanese ceramics and tea-ceremony utensils. Some outstanding examples of Bizen pottery and ancient ceramics are on display, and outside there is a lovely mossy garden with a bamboo grove, maple trees and a teahouse.

OWAKUDANI

Travel on to **Sounzan**, catching the cable car called the **Hakone Ropeway** for a giddy 30-minute journey over the mountains to Lake Ashino. If the weather is clear (it often isn't, particularly during the summer months), you will be able to get a good view of Mount Fuji (Fuji-san) during the journey.

Be sure to get off at the first stop, **Owakudani** ❻ ('great boiling hell'), a bleached terrain so barren-looking you could be forgiven for thinking you had been put down on a dead planet. Hakone has a history of volcanic erup-

tions, and the stench of sulphur and clouds of steam from the fumaroles at Owakudani are a constant reminder of how unstable the ground beneath you is. Locals boil eggs in the sulphur pits and then sell them to visitors with the unlikely assurance that by eating one your life will be extended by seven years.

AROUND LAKE ASHINO

The cable car terminates at **Togendai**, at the northern end of **Lake Ashino** ❼ (Ashino-ko) where, for the next stage of your journey, you should board one of the colourful mock-galleons that ply between here and Hakone-Machi. The boats are outrageously kitsch, but the journey across this serene lake is magical.

Hakone Barrier
You will disembark from the boat at **Hakone-machi**, which is the site of the **Hakone Barrier** ❽ (Hakone Sekisho; daily 9am–4.30pm), a replica of the original checkpoint that stood here during the Edo period. The barrier marks an important point on the Tokaido Road that ran between Kyoto and Edo (Tokyo). An exhibition hall beside the barrier provides the historical background to the road. A 1km (0.6-mile) section of the original Tokaido makes for a pleasant walk from the barrier, under tall cryptomeria trees, to the lakeside village of Moto-Hakone.

A galleon on Lake Ashino and the Hakone Gongen's red torii

Hakone Gongen

As you approach **Moto-Hakone**, you will get a lovely view of a red *torii* gate, which stands in the water and is framed by forest as well as, if you are lucky, the glorious backdrop of Mount Fuji. The gate is part of the shrine known as **Hakone Gongen** . Hidden among trees close to the shore, the shrine was founded in 757 and was once a popular place for samurai to pray.

HATAJUKU

Buses run from Moto-Hakone back to Hakone-Yumoto for the return journey to Tokyo. Alternatively, you can make the 11km (7-mile) hike through the forests, tracing the route of the Tokaido via the village of **Hatajuku** , which is famous for its woodwork craftsmen who specialise in marquetry.

Along the way you can pause, just as pilgrims of old did, at the still functioning **Amazake-jaya Teahouse**, where you can sample *amazake*, which is a sweet and mildly alcoholic milky rice drink.

TENZAN NOTEMBURO

About 2km (1.25 miles) from Hakone-Yumoto, the Tokaido hiking path passes the luxurious *onsen* complex **Tenzan Notemburo** (daily 9am–10pm). The bathing here is segregated, with indoor and outdoor pools designed in attractive arrangements of wood and rock. Men also have access to a clay sauna hut. You can dine here as well, see , before walking or catching the complimentary shuttle bus back to Hakone-Yumoto Station.

Food and drink

① KIKKA-SO-INN

Fujiya Hotel, Miyanoshita; tel: 0460-822 211; www.fujiyahotel.jp; ¥¥¥
While the Fujiya's other restaurants and lounges closed for renovations, this atmospheric restaurant, originally built as a royal villa in 1895, stayed open. It serves exquisitely prepared *kaiseki* cuisine, presented in beautiful wooden boxes traditional to Hakone.

② BELLA FORESTA

Hakone Open-Air Museum, Ninotaira, Hakone-machi; tel: 0460-821 161; www.hakone-oam.or.jp; daily 10am–3.30pm; ¥¥
The museum's buffet restaurant offers a wide range of Japanese and Western dishes, but if none of them suit there's also Chokoku-no-Mori, serving curries, pasta dishes and sandwiches, and a café serving coffees, cakes and ice creams and occupying a lovely spot overlooking the gardens.

③ TENZAN NOTEMBURO

208 Yumoto-Chaya, Hakone-Yumoto; tel: 0460-864 126; www.hakone.or.jp; ¥¥
The *onsen* complex is also an excellent place to eat after taking a bath. Its three restaurants serve *shabu shabu* (sautéed beef) and *teppanyaki* (grilled meat dishes), as well as humble bowls of noodles.

The Tosho-gu temple complex

NIKKO

Set off early for a full day's exploration of the opulent shrines and mausoleums of the early shoguns in the verdant hills of Nikko. Pack an overnight bag if you also wish to visit nearby Lake Chuzenji.

DISTANCE: 128km (80 miles) north from Tokyo to Nikko; walking tour: 3.5km (2.25 miles)

TIME: 1 or 2 days

START/END: Shin-kyo Bridge

POINTS TO NOTE: Although Nikko is accessible by JR trains, most people come here on the Tobu-Nikko line from Asakusa in Tokyo; in Nikko the JR and Tobu stations are beside each other. Tobu's Spacia limited express takes 1 hour 55 min, the cheaper *kyuko* service an extra 15 min. If you opt for the latter, be sure to sit in one of the first two carriages, as some of the trains divide at Shimo Imaichi Station, the stop before Nikko. If you are planning to include a visit to Lake Chuzenji, buy the All Nikko Pass (¥4,520 mid-April to November, ¥4,120 December–mid-April); for details about the pass and train times, see www. tobu.co.jp/foreign. In Nikko frequent local buses from the train stations allow you to skip the 20-minute walk up the town's somewhat shabby high street towards the shrine complex.

An *onsen* (hot-spring) resort in the mountains of Tochigi Prefecture, Nikko is best known as the location of the Tosho-gu shrine and mausoleum.

There's an information desk (daily 8.30am–5pm) in Tobu Nikko Station, while the main tourist office (www.nikko-japan. org; daily 9am–5pm) is midway along the main road from the station to Tosho-gu.

TOSHO-GU

The shrine **Tosho-gu** was built to honour Tokugawa Ieyasu, the shogun who unified Japan around 1600 and founded a political dynasty that lasted for over 250 years. Some 1,500 craftsmen and artists were brought to Nikko for a period of two years by Tokugawa Iemitsu, Ieyasu's grandson and the third shogun. The shrine was completed in 1634 to a mixed reception. Some considered it to be a fitting tribute to Japan's greatest shogun; others regarded it as a gaudy extravagance, more expressive of Chinese Tang-dynasty tastes and too much of a deviation from the simple, understated design of most Shinto shrines. Regardless, the complex received

X Shin-kyo, the Sacred Bridge that marks the entrance to Tosho-gu

Unesco World Heritage Status in 2004 and is always inundated with visitors.

Shin-kyo Bridge

Marking the entrance to Tosho-gu's grounds is the vermilion-painted **Shin-kyo** ❶ (Sacred Bridge; Apr–Sep 8am–5pm, Oct–mid-Nov 8am–4pm, mid-Nov–Mar 9am–4pm) over the Daiya River. In former times, only the shogun and imperial messengers were allowed to cross the wooden bridge, which is best viewed from the road rather than close up.

Rinno-ji

Cross the road from the bridge and follow the steps of a path that winds up to a **statue of Shodo Shonin**, the priest who founded Nikko more than 1,200 years ago when the mountains in this area were honoured as gods. Close by is the site of **Rinno-ji** ❷ (daily Apr–Oct 8am–4.30pm, Nov–Mar 8am–3.30pm), a temple which Shodo founded in 766. The temple's main hall, the **Sanbutsu-do**, enshrines three huge wood-carved and gilded statues: a thousand-armed Kannon, the Amida Buddha and a horse-headed Kannon. A separate ticket gains you entrance to Rinno-ji's **Treasure House** and **Shoyo-en**, a classic, landscaped stroll garden that was completed in 1815.

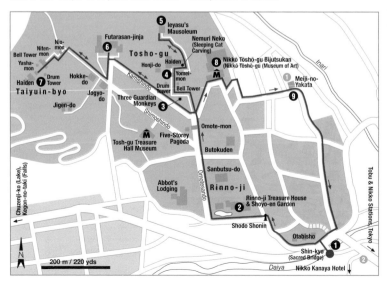

Lake Chuzenji to the west of Nikko

Exit Rinno-ji onto broad Omote-sando, the main approach to Tosho-gu's original stone *torii* gate. A five-storey pagoda stands to the left, an example of how Buddhism and Shinto are blended here. Ascend another set of stone steps and pass through **Omote-mon**, Tosho-gu's entrance gate (daily Apr–Oct 8am–4.30pm, Nov–Mar 8am–3.30pm), to reach the area containing the sacred storehouses and stable, and the carving of **Three Guardian Monkeys** ❸ in their famous pose, 'See no evil, hear no evil, speak no evil'. The next terrace contains stone lan-terns donated by *daimyo* (feudal lords) from all over Japan. A large revolving bronze lantern, with the Tokugawa family crest mistakenly engraved upside down, is a gift from Holland, the only country in the 17th century allowed limited diplomatic and trade relations with Japan.

Yomei-mon

The lavish gate **Yomei-mon** ❹ stands at the top of a short flight of steps to the upper terrace. Carved and gilded with more than 400 images of flowers, dragons, birds and Chinese sages, it is also known as the Twilight Gate because of the risk that you will become so mesmerised by it that you will spend the whole day there. To the gate's left, behind a drum tower, there's the **Hon-ji-do**, famous for its huge 'roaring dragon' ceiling painting. If you stand under its head and clap, you will hear the dragon roar.

Ieyasu's Mausoleum

Having passed through the Yomei-mon, most visitors turn right and continue up to Ieyasu's Mausoleum. As you leave the shrine, look out for a small carving on the lintel. This is the sleeping cat *(nemuri neko)* carving, which has become Nikko's mascot.

In contrast to the flamboyance of the shrine, there is a more sacred air to **Ieyasu's Mausoleum** ❺ (charge), surrounded by cryptomeria trees and reached by 200 steps.

Lake Chuzenji

A visit to Lake Chuzenji (Chuzenji-ko) and the spectacular Kegon Falls (Kegon-no-taki), located 10km (6 miles) west of Nikko, is highly recommended. The lake is reached via the Iroha Slope, a road with scenic views from a series of hairpin bends, each one named after a different phonetic character in the Japanese alphabet. Both Chuzenji village and the tiny hot-spring resort of Yumoto, located on a plateau surrounded by mountains a short distance from Lake Chuzenji, offer plenty of accommodation should you wish to stay here and enjoy the spectacular scenery and natural surroundings. The bus ride up to Lake Chuzenji from Nikko takes 50 minutes. However, in autumn the journey can take up to three times longer.

Three Guardian Monkeys

FUTARASAN-JINJA

Retrace your route to the exit of Tosho-gu, bear right at the pagoda and walk along a path lined with stone lanterns to reach the grounds of **Futarasan-jinja** ❻. Dedicated to nearby Mount Nantai, the simplicity of this red, lacquered shrine and its pleasant garden is a welcome relief after the highly accomplished but ostentatious shrine of Tosho-gu. You can enjoy a bowl of *matcha* here, the frothy green brew made during the tea ceremony. The grounds of the shrine contain a famous bronze *bakemono toro* (phantom lantern), cast in 1292. According to legend, the lantern used to roam the shrine precincts at night, terrorising its night watchmen.

TAIYUIN-BYO

Just beyond the Futarasan Shrine is the attractive **Taiyuin-byo** ❼ (daily Apr–Oct 8am–4.30pm, Nov–Mar 8am–3.30pm), the mausoleum of Tokugawa Iemitsu. It's intentionally less ostentatious than Tosho-gu and usually a lot less crowded.

NIKKO TOSHO-GU MUSEUM OF ART

From Taiyuin-byo return to Omote-mon and, facing away from Tosho-gu, take the left path leading to the **Nikko Tosho-gu Museum of Art** ❽ (Nikko Tosho-gu Bijutsukan; Apr–Oct 8am–5pm, Nov–Mar 8am–4pm). The collection of painted screens and sliding doors, housed in a wooden building erected in 1928, is one of the finest exhibitions of its kind in Japan.

MEIJI-NO-YAKATA

Next to the museum are the grounds of **Meiji-no-Yakata** ❾, an early 20th-century Western-style holiday villa. It now houses several restaurants including, to the rear of the main building, the vegetarian **Gyoshintei**, see ❶. Alternatively, it's a short walk back to the Shin-kyo Bridge and main road, along which you will find both the historic Nikko Kanaya Hotel and the simple eatery **Hippari Dako**, see ❷.

Food and drink

❶ GYOSHINTEI

2339-1 Sannai; tel: 0288-533 751; daily noon–8pm; ¥¥¥
Behind the Western-style restaurant Meiji-no-Yakata is this traditional place where you sit on *tatami* mats and gaze at a lovely garden while eating a *shojin-ryori* vegetarian banquet.

❷ HIPPARI DAKO

1011 Kami-hatsuishicho; tel: 0288-532 933; daily 11am–8pm; ¥
On the main road up to the Shin-kyo Bridge is this eternally popular café, serving noodles and *yakitori* (skewers of grilled chicken) and plastered with the business cards of thousands of visitors.

DIRECTORY

Hand-picked hotels and restaurants to suit all budgets and tastes, organised by area, plus select nightlife listings, an alphabetical listing of practical information, a language guide and an overview of the best books and films to give you a flavour of the city.

A suite at the Mandarin Oriental

ACCOMMODATION

There is no lack of places to stay in Tokyo, with some of the world's top brands in the market and more on the way for the Tokyo 2020 Summer Olympics. Accommodation ranges from deluxe palaces to no-frills business lodgings and budget 'capsule hotels'. Older establishments exude a distinctive Japanese ambience, while business hotels come with clean and functional bedrooms.

The best traditional Japanese inns, or *ryokan*, epitomise the essence of Japanese hospitality. You sleep on futon mattresses on *tatami* mats, bathe in a traditional bath and are served exquisite *kaiseki ryori* meals in your room by attendants in kimonos. Note that they often don't accept credit cards; if staying at one, it is best to check in advance.

Capsule hotels have become a famous symbol of crowded Japan. Located near big stations, they provide fully equipped sleeping cells at economic rates, mostly for drunken men who miss the last train home to the suburbs.

Airbnb and other sharing economy approaches to accommodations have recently arrived in Japan. Potential guests are advised that legal issues with Japan's Inns and Hotel Act remain to be sorted out.

Western-style hotels charge on a per-room basis, although at traditional ryokan inns and pensions customers are charged per person with the rate usually including dinner and breakfast. Many larger hotels also offer non-smoking rooms and women-only floors. All hotel rates include 8 percent consumption tax. Luxury hotels may impose a 10–15 percent service charge. If your room costs over ¥10,000 per person per night, there's also a Tokyo Metropolitan Government tax of ¥100 per person per night (¥200 per person if the room costs over ¥15,000). This tax is set to be suspended during the Olympic and Paralympic Games, from July to September 2020.

Marunouchi and Ginza

Aman Tokyo
The Otemachi Tower, 1-5-6 Otemachi; tel 5224 3333; www.aman.com/resorts/aman-tokyo; station: Otemachi; ¥¥¥¥
Uber luxury hotel atop a sleek new tower in Tokyo's business district, offering all the amenities one expects of this chain catering to the one percent.

Diamond Hotel
25 Ichibancho, Chiyoda-ku; tel: 3263 2211; station: Hanzomon; ¥¥

Price for a double room for one night without breakfast:
¥¥¥¥ = over ¥30,000
¥¥¥ = ¥20,000–30,000
¥¥ = ¥10,000–20,000
¥ = below ¥10,000

The Peninsula Tokyo

Just minutes from the Imperial Palace and the British Embassy. Nice quiet area.

Hotel Intergate

3-7-8 Kyobashi; tel: 5524 2929; station: Takaracho; ¥¥

Relaxed, modern hotel with comfortable, no-frills guestrooms, healthy buffet breakfasts and some lovely communal spaces, including a library full of photographic and reference books and a gallery stocked with traditional arts and crafts.

Imperial Hotel

1-1-1 Uchisaiwai-cho, Chiyoda-ku; tel: 3504 1111; www.imperialhotel.co.jp; station: Hibiya; ¥¥¥¥

Japan's first Western-style hotel (1890), now in its third incarnation, offers top service and restful rooms. Its central location near Hibiya Park, the Imperial Palace and the chic Ginza shopping area makes it a favourite of travellers and businesspeople alike.

Mandarin Oriental Tokyo

2-1-1 Nihonbashi Marunouchi, Chuo-ku; tel: 3270 8800; www.mandarinoriental.com/tokyo; station: Mitsukoshi-Mae; ¥¥¥¥

Hong Kong luxury chain's centrally located Tokyo outpost boasts no less than three Michelin star-rated restaurants and an award-winning spa.

Mitsui Garden

8-13-1 Ginza, Chuo-ku; tel: 3543 1131; www.gardenhotels.co.jp/ginza-premier; station: Tsukijishijo; ¥¥¥

Sleek, modern hotel with comfortable guestrooms, many offering impressive views from the higher floors of Ginza's tallest high-rise. The aptly named Sky Restaurant sits on the 16th floor and serves Western breakfasts and *kaiseki* dinners, while the stylish Karin Bar has live jazz, cocktails, and a beautiful bar made from a 600-year-old karin tree.

Palace Hotel

1-1-1 Marunouchi, Chiyoda-ku; tel: 3211 5211; en.palacehoteltokyo.com; station: Otemachi or Tokyo; ¥¥¥

Well-established hotel with spacious, renovated guest rooms and a calmer ambience than other top hotels. Upper levels allow prime views of the Imperial Palace grounds. So does the Crown Restaurant on the top floor, a popular place to spend an evening. The interior, despite the sweeping views, can seem a little gloomy at times.

The Peninsula Tokyo

1-8-1 Yurakucho, Chiyoda-ku; tel: 6270 2888; www.peninsula.com; stations: Hibiya or Yurakucho; ¥¥¥¥

A branch of the Hong Kong flagship, the Peninsula's superb location and high-class style are hard to match. Try to get one of the middle- or upper-level rooms, which have outstanding views.

Yaesu Terminal Hotel

1-5-14 Yaesu, Chuo-ku; tel: 3281 3771; www.yth.jp; station: Tokyo; ¥¥

The rooms in this business hotel may be on the small side, but they are clean and good value for the area.

Roppongi and Akasaka

Akasaka Excel Hotel Tokyu

2-14-3 Nagatacho, Chiyoda-ku; tel: 3580 2311; www.tokyuhotelsjapan.com; station: Akasaka-Mitsuke; ¥¥¥

Offers reliable quality, efficient service and reasonable rates compared to the nearby luxury hotels. Rooms away from the road are quieter. There are good shops and restaurants in the downstairs mall, and bars on the upper levels.

Akasaka Yoko Hotel

6-14-12 Akasaka, Minato-ku; tel: 3586 4050; www.yokohotel.co.jp; station: Akasaka; ¥¥

The friendly Yoko is well positioned for visits not only to Roppongi's restaurants, galleries and night-time entertainment, but also to two famous Shinto shrines: Nogi and Hie. Though not large, the rooms are affordable, clean and comfortable, with internet connections.

ANA Tokyo

1-12-33 Akasaka, Minato-ku; tel: 3505 1111; www.anaintercontinental-tokyo.jp; station: Tameike-Sanno; ¥¥¥¥

This five-star hotel owned by All Nippon Airways is set in Ark Hills, an office and shopping complex close to the business and entertainment districts (and the interminable drone of the Shuto Expressway), just two minutes' walk from the subway station. The huge, brightly lit lobby is a foretaste of the large rooms; those on the upper storeys have great views.

Arca Torre

6-1-23 Roppongi, Minato-ku; tel: 3404 5111; www.arktower.jp/arcatorre; station: Roppongi; ¥¥

Close to the busy Roppongi Crossing, this place can be a little noisy at times and is certainly at the heart of the action. Standard single rooms boast large semi-double beds, and there are helpful multilingual staff.

Asia Center of Japan Hotel

8-10-32 Akasaka, Minato-ku; tel: 3402 6111; www.asiacenter.or.jp; station: Nogizaka; ¥

Book well ahead for this popular lodging for low-budget travellers. Rooms in the newer wing are a notch up from the older cramped ones. A few minutes' walk from the subway, the location is good for both the Roppongi and Aoyoma areas.

Grand Hyatt

6-10-3 Roppongi, Minato-ku; tel: 4333 1234; http://tokyo.grand.hyatt. com; station: Roppongi; ¥¥¥¥

Truly spectacular, but in an understated manner. Wood, glass and marble in the public areas form clutter-free and contemporary lines. Bedrooms feature flat-

screen televisions (including one in the bathroom) and high-speed internet, plus capacious bathrooms.

Hotel Villa Fontaine Roppongi
1-6-2 Roppongi, Minato-ku; tel: 3560 1110; www.hvf.jp; station: Roppongi-itchome; ¥¥
One in the chain of excellent-value, stylish business hotels. Offers rooms larger than most in this category, a complimentary buffet breakfast and discounted rates at weekends.

New Otani
4-1 Kioi-cho, Chiyoda-ku; tel: 3265 1111; www.newotani.co.jp; station: Akasaka; ¥¥¥¥
A massive complex with many restaurants and extensive Japanese gardens that are worth seeing in their own right. On the borderline with Akasaka, but within a 10-minute walk of the Imperial Palace, the location is ideal for both sightseeing and nightlife.

Okura
2-10-4 Toranomon, Minato-ku; tel: 3582 0111; www.okura.com; station: Roppongi-Itchome; ¥¥¥¥
A revered classic of subdued 1960s Japanese modernism, the Okura was controversially demolished in 2015, with a bland if high-tech replacement tower to open in 2019 in time for the 2020 Olympics.

Presso Inn Akasaka
6-2-1 Akasaka, Minato-ku; tel: 5562 0077; www.presso-inn.com; station: Akasaka; ¥¥
Professionally run hotel catering to business and leisure travellers, with compact, contemporary guestrooms, decent international breakfasts and a great location a stone's throw from Akasaka station.

Remm Roppongi
14-4-7 Roppongi, Minato-ku; tel: 6863 0606; http://global.hankyu-hotel.com/remm-roppongi; station: Roppongi; ¥¥
Offering good value amid Roppongi's often expensive accommodation options, this modern three-star has comfortable, if rather bland, guestrooms, cool monochrome bathrooms that match the sleek exterior, and a well-regarded chophouse and bar.

Ritz Carlton
Tokyo Midtown, 9-7-1 Akasaka, Minato-ku; tel: 3423 8000; www.ritzcarlton.com; station: Roppongi; ¥¥¥¥
Occupying the top nine floors of the Midtown Tower is this ultra-luxury hotel. Beautifully decorated and spacious rooms are complemented by the Ritz's famous afternoon teatime service, with bird's-eye views of Tokyo from the Lobby Lounge and Bar on the 45th floor.

Shiba Park Hotel
1-5-10 Shiba-Koen, Minato-ku; tel: 3433 4141; www.shibaparkhotel.com; station: Onarimon; ¥¥

The stunning view from the Park Hyatt's New York Grill

A little-known hotel, despite its attractive location just four minutes from the Onarimon subway and the impressive Sangedatsu Gate leading into Zojo-ji Temple. Quiet and cosy, and the staff here are helpful and attentive.

Aoyama

Tokyu Stay Aoyama

2-27-1 Minami-Aoyama, Minato-ku; tel: 3497 0109; www.tokyustay.co.jp; station: Gaienmae; ¥¥

Aoyama is short on hotels, but this one, a short walk from Aoyama Park, is worth searching out. It offers good-quality Western-style rooms, many with washer/driers and kitchenettes, and pleasant service.

Shibuya

Capsule Hotel Shibuya

1-19-14 Dogenzaka, Shibuya-ku; tel: 3464 1777; station: Shibuya; ¥

A 15-minute walk from the station, this capsule hotel might be a last resort, or a once-in-a-lifetime experience. Adequate facilities: communal showers, capsule TVs, coin lockers, a restaurant and vending machines dispensing beer and noodles. Men only.

Cerulean Tower Tokyu Hotel

26-1 Sakuragaoka-cho, Shibuya-ku; tel: 3476 3000; www.ceruleantower-hotel.com; station: Shibuya; ¥¥¥¥

Shibuya's most upmarket hotel covers the 19th to 37th floors of a tower, offering splendid views. The rooms are spacious, fully equipped and tastefully decorated. On the premises are bars and several Japanese and Western eating options, including a modern *kaiseki ryori* restaurant and *noh* theatre.

Nadeshiko Hotel

10-5, Shinsen-cho, Shibuya-ku; tel: 5489 3667; station: Shibuya; ¥

Long considered the sole preserve of men, Tokyo's capsule hotels are finally beginning to address the unbalance with an increasing number of women-only establishments. This modern hotel includes a communal bathhouse and traditional Japanese restaurant.

Shibuya Creston Hotel

10-8 Kamiyamacho, Shibuya-ku; tel: 3481 5800; www.crestonhotel.jp/shibuya; station: Shibuya; ¥¥¥

An intimate boutique hotel stashed in the quiet, posh Kamiyamacho backstreets 15 minutes from Shibuya Station. Also near Bunkamura.

Shibuya Excel Tokyu

1-12-2 Dogenzaka, Shibuya-ku; tel: 5457 0109; www.tokyuhotelsjapan.com; station: Shibuya; ¥¥

This well-priced hotel for business travellers is part of the Mark City complex attached to Shibuya Station. It offers one floor solely for women, as well as a bar, restaurants and all the amenities you would expect from this hotel chain.

Even the hotel's bathrooms have great views

Shibuya Hotel En

1-1 Maruyamacho, Shibuya-ku; tel: 5489 1010; station: Shibuya; ¥¥

This small business hotel, under 10 minutes from Shibuya Station and opposite the Bunkamura complex, is ideally located for taking in the arts, shopping and nightlife of Shibuya.

Shinjuku

HI Tokyo Central Youth Hostel

Central Plaza, 18F, 21-1 Kagurakashi, Shinjuku-ku; tel: 3235 1107; www.hihostels. com/hostels/tokyo-hi-tokyo-central-yh; station: Iidabashi; ¥

If you don't mind sharing a room, the clean dormitory-style bunk beds at this eco-friendly youth hostel right next to JR Iidabashi Station may suit. There's no access to the building between 10am and 3pm, and also an 11pm curfew.

Hotel Wing International

1-21-7 Kabuki-cho, Shinjuku-ku; tel: 3200 0122; www.hotelwing.co.jp; station: Shinjuku; ¥

Rooms here are not the most stylish or modern, but they're clean and comfortable, everything works, and you're right in the heart of the action. There's also decent Japanese and Western food on offer at the restaurant.

Hyatt Regency Tokyo

2-7-2 Nishi-Shinjuku, Shinjuku-ku; tel: 3348 1234; www.tokyo.regency.hyatt.com; stations: Shinjuku or Tochomae; ¥¥¥¥

In the heart of West Shinjuku, this is one of Tokyo's most praised hotels, although you wouldn't realise it from the outside. The interior, with its soaring atrium lobby, is a different story. The posh executive floors are exclusive, with separate facilities and king-sized beds.

Kadoya Hotel

1-23-1 Nishi-Shinjuku, Shinjuku-ku; tel: 3346 2561; www.kadoya-hotel.co.jp; stations: Shinjuku or Tochomae; ¥¥

A super business hotel that's a bargain for the location. There's internet access, a good *izakaya* (restaurant-pub) in the basement and English-speaking staff.

Keio Plaza Hotel

2-2-1 Nishi-Shinjuku, Shinjuku-ku; tel: 3344 0111; www.keioplaza.com; stations: Shinjuku or Tochomae; ¥¥¥

This large 45-storey skyscraper in West Shinjuku is long established and well maintained, with a health club, outdoor swimming pool, business facilities and an array of fine restaurants and bars.

Park Hyatt Tokyo

3-7-1-2 Nishi-Shinjuku, Shinjuku-ku; tel: 5322 1234; www.tokyo.park.hyatt.com; station: Tochomae; ¥¥¥¥

Made famous when the movie *Lost in Translation* was shot here, this deluxe property has a fantastic setting on the top 14 floors of the 52-storey Park Tower. Expect top-class facilities and superb service. Home to the excellent New York Grill restaurant.

Capsule hotel

Shinjuku Prince Hotel

1-30-1 Kabuki-cho, Shinjuku-ku; tel: 3205 1111; www.princehotels.com; station: Shinjuku; ¥¥

Look down from your room at the goings-on in Kabuki-cho, the heart of Shinjuku nightlife. Right next to Shinjuku Station, the location may not be picturesque, but there is never a dull moment in this exciting part of town. Adequate rooms, good facilities. The restaurant on the 25th floor has the best views this side of Shinjuku.

Yanaka and Ueno

Ryokan Katsutaro Annex

3-8-4 Yanaka, Taito-ku; tel: 3828 2500; www.katsutaro.com/annex_accom.html; station: Sendagi; ¥¥

This modern *ryokan* exhibits classic Japanese design, with *tatami* flooring and paper-screen windows. There are also private bathrooms and broadband internet access in each room, along with free internet usage and coffee in the entrance area. The hotel is located just around the corner from Yanaka Ginza, a lively street with craft and tea shops.

Sawanoya Ryokan

2-3-11 Yanaka, Taito-ku; tel: 3822 2251; www.sawanoya.com; station: Nezu; ¥

This friendly, family-run *ryokan*, situated in a residential neighbourhood close to the old quarter of *Yanaka*, offers small but comfortable rooms with *tatami* mats. The ¥300 self-service breakfast is good value. It's about a seven-minute walk from Nezu Station.

Ueno First City Hotel

1-14-8 Ueno, Taito-ku; tel: 3831 8215; www.uenocity-hotel.com; station: Yushima; ¥¥

This smart business hotel with a red-brick façade prides itself on its comfort and efficiency. It's located within walking distance of both Ueno and the area around the Yushima Tenjin shrine. The restaurant, bar and coffee shop are as intimate as the cosy guestrooms.

Ikebukuro and Mejirodai

Chinzan-so Hotel

Chinzan-so, 2-10-8 Sekiguchi, Bunkyo-ku; tel: 3943 2222; www.hotel-chinzanso-tokyo.com; station: Edogawabashi; ¥¥¥¥

A superlative low-rise hotel overlooking the woodlands of the Chinzan-so garden, with its pagoda, waterfall and Buddhist statuary. Western luxury is combined with Japanese attention to detail. A drawback is the rather remote location, a 10-minute walk from Edogawabashi Station.

Hotel Metropolitan

1-6-1 Nishi-Ikebukuro, Toshima-ku; tel: 3980 1111; www.hotelmetropolitan.jp; station: Ikebukuro; ¥¥¥

A plush hotel with comfortable, good-sized rooms, several restaurants and an outdoor pool (mid-June–early Sept).

A top view over Ikebukuro

Kimi Ryokan

2-36-8 Ikebukuro, Toshima-ku; tel: 3971 3766; www.kimi-ryokan.jp; station: Ikebukuro; ¥

This homely *ryokan* is one of Tokyo's best-loved budget stays, with helpful English-speaking staff. It's very popular, so book in advance. Located in a quiet backstreet off Tokiwa-dori, the ryokan is a 10-minute walk to the JR station.

Sunshine City

Grand Prince Hotel

New Takanawa, 3-13-1 Takanawa, Minato-ku; tel: 3442 1111; www.princehotels.com; station: Shinagawa, ¥¥¥

One in a complex of three Prince hotels all in the same beautifully landscaped gardens. The facilities are excellent, the rooms luxurious and spacious. The service is highly reputed. Guests at one of the Prince buildings can use facilities in the other two. Located in an affluent residential district, there is not much nightlife in this area. It is, however, only five minutes from the JR station.

Hotel Excellent Ebisu

1-9-5 Ebisu-Nishi, Minato-ku; tel: 5458 0087; station: Ebisu; ¥¥

Nothing fancy about this hotel with its plain, rather small rooms and only basic facilities. Besides its helpful staff and attractive rates, its location near the Yamanote Line, just one stop from Shibuya, with access to trendy Ebisu, makes it popular. It is good for exploring the western reaches of Tokyo. Close to Ebisu Station's west exit.

Hotel Gajoen

1-8-1 Shimo Meguro, Meguro-ku; tel: 3491 4111; www.hotelgajoen-tokyo.com; station: Meguro; ¥¥¥¥

A very old and beautiful ryokan, the traditional lodgings here are very expensive. Lovely gardens, artwork and a refined atmosphere add to the sublime experience. European and Japanese-style rooms available; ask for the latter. Only a three-minute walk from the JR station.

Keikyu Ex Hotel

4-10-8 Takanawa, Minato-ku; tel: 5423 3910; www.keikyu-exhotel.jp; station: Shinagawa; ¥¥

Monolithic hotel near Shinagawa station, with functional, comfortable rooms, with Japanese/Western breakfasts, and no end of restaurants, shops and bars within easy reach.

Prince Hotel

3-1-5 Higashi-Ikebukuro, Toshima-ku; tel: 3988 1111; www.princehotels.com; station: Ikebukuro; ¥¥

Efficient, well run and well equipped with business facilities. Conveniently located in the Sunshine City complex, with its array of shops and restaurants. JR station is an eight-minute walk away.

Nikko Tokyo's exterior

Sansuiso Ryokan

2-9-5 Higashi-Gotanda, Shinagawa-ku; tel: 3441 7475; www.sansuiso.net; station: Gotanda; ¥

Cosy ryokan conveniently located five minutes from Gotanda Station. Traditional Japanese-style rooms that offer a choice of private or shared facilities.

Sheraton Miyako Hotel Tokyo

1-1-50 Shiroganedai, Minato-ku; tel: 3447 3111; www.miyakohotels.ne.jp; station: Shirokaneda; ¥¥¥

Affiliated with Kyoto's famous Miyako Hotel, this Tokyo equivalent successfully attempts to replicate the prototype. Located in a pleasant, quiet neighbourhood near the Happo-en Garden and the National Park for Nature Study, this location makes for a lovely retreat. Only 10 minutes from Shirokanedai subway station.

Westin Hotel Tokyo

1-4-1 Mita, Meguro-ku; tel: 5423 7000; www.marriott.com; station: Ebisu; ¥¥¥¥

Spacious guest rooms, sophisticated interiors, personalised service and a peaceful setting opposite a fake chateau (housing a restaurant) and the soaring office blocks of Yebisu Garden Place. The Westin models itself on grand European-style hotels, offering gracefully designed rooms, an elegant lobby and tastefully decorated public spaces.

Asakusa View Hotel

3-17-1 Nishi-Asakusa, Taito-ku; tel: 3847 1111; www.viewhotels.co.jp/asakusa; station: Asakusa; ¥¥

Well situated for sightseeing and shopping in downtown Asakusa, this hotel has Western-style rooms that offer good views – as does the bar on the 28th floor.

Ryokan Shigetsu

1-31-11 Asakusa, Taito-ku; tel: 3843 2345; www.shigetsu.com; station: Asakusa; ¥¥

Steps away from Nakamise-dori, this is one of Asakusa's nicest ryokan offerings, with small Western- or Japanese-style rooms, all en suite. The top-floor bath offers views over the nearby temple roofs.

Sukeroku-no-yado Sadachiyo

2-20-1 Asakusa, Taito-ku; tel: 3842 6431; www.sadachiyo.co.jp; stations: Asakusa or Tawaramachi; ¥¥

Close by Senso-ji, this is an atmospheric *ryokan* where the traditions of old Edo are maintained. All the *tatami* rooms have en-suite bathrooms, but there are also traditional-style larger communal baths.

Conrad Hotel

1-9-1 Higashi-Shimbashi, Minato-ku; tel: 6388 8000; www.conradtokyo.co.jp; station: Shimbashi; ¥¥¥¥

Waterfront views at Nikko Tokyo

Shiodome's high-end accommodation doesn't come more luxurious than this. Immaculate service from multilingual staff, designer rooms with hardwood finishing and views across the Hama-Rikyu Garden and Tokyo Bay. It's also within walking distance of Tsukiji Outer Market.

Hilton Tokyo Odaiba
1-9-1 Daiba, Minato-ku; tel: 5500 5500; www.hilton.com; station: Odaiba; ¥¥¥¥
Smack-bang in front of Odaiba Station on the Yurikamome Line, and a stroll up from the leisure complexes of Palette Town and Aqua City, the Hilton has one of the best views of the waterfront. The terrace restaurant and Captain's Bar are romantic settings popular with couples. First-rate service and food. Convenient access to all Odaiba sights.

Tokyo Bay Ariake Washington Hotel
3-7-1 Ariake, Koto-ku; tel: 5564 0111; en.washington-hotels.jp; station: Ariake; ¥¥
A comfortable business hotel on Odaiba, this has the same facilities as you would find in its other branches, but this one, at 20 storeys, is one of the larger buildings. There are several Western and Japanese restaurants on site. It's popular with those attending exhibitions at the Tokyo Big Sight venue next door. Located just a short walk away from Ariake Station.

Tokyo Bayside InterContinental
Tokyo Bay, 1-16-2 Kaigan, Minato-ku; tel: 5404 2222; www.interconti-tokyo.com; station: Takeshiba; ¥¥¥¥
Overlooking the mouth of the Sumida River and Tokyo waterfront, all its rooms have panoramic views of Odaiba Island and Rainbow Bridge. Rooms are spacious and stylishly appointed. The hotel is part of a complex that faces the east exit of Takeshiba station; a short walk to the Hama-Rikyu Garden.

Chilled udon noodles with shredded seaweed and grated daikon radish

RESTAURANTS

Most restaurants close between lunch and dinner. English-language menus are not common, but many eateries have plastic food displays in their windows. For up-to-date information on Tokyo's dynamic restaurant scene, check out the Tokyo Food Page (www.bento.com) or the reviews in The Japan Times (www.japantimes.co.jp) and *Metropolis* (http://metropolisjapan.com). Yelp and Trip Advisor can also be useful sources of information.

Marunouchi and Ginza

Andy's Shin-Hinomoto

2-4-4 Yurakucho, Chiyoda-ku; tel: 3214 8021; www.andysfish.com; Mon–Sat 5pm–midnight; station: Yurakucho; ¥

Also known as Andy's Fish, this noisy, friendly no-nonsense *izakaya* (tavern) is built under the railway tracks, serving fresh seafood at reasonable prices. British owner presides over his Japanese family's establishment. English-speaking. Cash only. Partially smoking.

Prices for a three-course meal, excluding beverages:

¥¥¥¥ = over ¥5,000
¥¥¥ = ¥3,000–5,000
¥¥ = ¥1,000–3,000
¥ = below ¥1,000

Aux Amis des Vins

2-5-6 Ginza, Chuo-ku; tel: 3567 4120; www.auxamis.com/desvins; Tue–Fri 11.20am–2pm and 5.30pm–midnight, Sat, Sun 11.30am–3pm and 5–11pm; station: Ginza; ¥¥¥

Good French cuisine in the middle ground between bistro and haute, in a casual setting, with an extensive wine cellar. Reservations advised. No smoking.

Bird Land

B1F Tsukamoto Sozan Building, 4-2-15 Ginza, Chuo-ku; tel: 5250 1081; http://ginza-birdland.sakura.ne.jp; Tue–Sat 5–9.30pm; station: Ginza; ¥¥¥

Top-quality *yakitori* (grilled skewers of chicken), made with free-range chicken grilled over charcoal. Don't miss the *sansai-yaki* (chicken breast grilled with Japanese pepper). Reservations advised. No smoking.

Dhaba India

2-7-9 Yaesu, Chuo-ku; tel: 3272 7160; www.dhabaindia.com/dhaba/index.html; Mon–Fri 11.15am–2.30pm and 5.30–10.30pm, Sat–Sun 11.30am–2.30pm and 5–9pm; station: Kyobashi; ¥¥

Fragrant curries, generous thali meals and masala dhosas. The best South Indian cuisine in the city. No smoking.

Elio Locanda Italiana

2-5-2 Kojimachi, Chiyoda-ku; tel: 3239

A seafood soup

6771; www.elio.co.jp/en; Mon–Sat 11.45am–2.15pm and 5.45–10.15pm; station: Hanzomon; ¥¥¥

Elio Orsara's fresh pasta, Calabrian country soups and excellent southern Italian food come highly recommended. No smoking.

Elio Locanda Italiana

8-7-10 Ginza, Chuo-ku; tel: 3572 2930; www.little-okinawa.co.jp; Mon–Fri 5pm–3am, Sat 5pm–midnight, Sun 4–11pm; station: Shinbashi; ¥¥

This cosy bar-restaurant showcases the food of subtropical Okinawa. Plenty of pork, stir-fries featuring bitter melon, and Chinese-style noodles, all washed down with potent awamori liquor. Service charge ¥500.

Ohmatsuya

7F, 5-6-13 Ginza, Chuo-ku; tel: 3571 7053; Mon–Sat 5.30–10pm; station: Ginza; ¥¥¥¥

Refined traditional fare in a rustic setting evoking rural Yamagata. Charcoal-grill beef and seafood at your table.

Otako Honten

2-2-3 Ginza, Chuo-ku; tel: 3243 8282; Mon–Fri 11.30am–1.30pm and 5pm–10.15pm, Sat 4pm–9.45pm; station: Ginza; ¥

Sit at the counter, sip sake and nibble on *oden* (fish, tofu, eggs and vegetables simmered in a savory broth): blue-collar comfort food. Cash only.

Rangetsu

3-5-8 Ginza, Chuo-ku; tel: 3567 1021; www.ginza-rangetsu.com/english/index.html; daily 11.30am–9.30pm; station: Ginza; ¥¥¥¥

Refined Japanese cuisine based around *shabu-shabu* (hotpot) and *sukiyaki* (one-pot meal), featuring premium Wagyu beef cooked at the table. Service charge 10 percent after 4pm. Partially non smoking.

Ten-Ichi Ginza Honten

6-6-5 Ginza, Chuo-ku; tel: 3571 1949; www.tenichi.co.jp; daily 11.30am–10pm; station: Ginza; ¥¥¥¥

Tokyo's best-known tempura house, serving high-end meals of deep-fried battered seafood and vegetables in a great ambience. No smoking.

Ten-mo

4-1-3 Nihombashi-Motomachi, Chuo-ku; tel: 3241 7035; www.tenmo.jp/e-index.html; Mon–Sat noon–2pm and 5–8pm; station: Nihonbashi; ¥¥¥

This old-style tempura shop prepares exquisite morsels of seafood and vegetables fried in rich sesame oil. The counter seats just six, so reservations are essential. No smoking.

Wattle

6F Shin-Marunouchi Building, 1-5-1 Marunouchi, Chiyoda-ku; tel: 5288 7828; Mon–Sat 11am–2.30pm and 5.30–10pm, Sun 5.30–9pm; station: Tokyo; ¥¥¥

Fresh sashimi

Opened in 2019, this stylish restaurant specialises in Australian-French fusion cuisine, with a particular focus on healthy, plant-based dishes. The botanic course (¥6,000) is a veggie extravaganza which showcases the best seasonal produce from the countryside around Tokyo. Partially no smoking.

Roppongi and Akasaka

Butagumi

2-24-9 Nishi-Azabu, Minato-ku; tel: 5466 6775; www.butagumi.com/nishiazabu/about.html; Tue–Sun 11.30am–2pm and 6pm–9.30pm; station: Roppongi; ¥¥

A traditional setting for one of Tokyo's finest renditions of *tonkatsu* – deep-fried, breaded premium pork cutlets. Choose fatty *rosu* or lean filet or Iberian. English spoken. No smoking.

Chinese Café Eight

2F, Court Annex, 3-2-13 Nishi-Azabu, Minato-ku; tel: 5414 5708; http://en.cceight.com; daily 24 hours; station: Roppongi; ¥¥

Budget Chinese diner open round the clock, serving Peking duck (for three or four people) dumplings and simple stir-fries at bargain prices. They also have branches in Ebisu and Akasaka.

Daigo

2F Forest Tower, 2-3-1 Atago, Minato-ku; tel: 3431 0811; http://atago-daigo.jp/en; daily 11.30am–2pm, 5–8pm; station: Onarimon; ¥¥¥¥

Buddhist temple cooking elevated to supreme levels of refinement. The extended vegetarian banquets feature 10–15 courses of exquisite complexity, served in private rooms. Allow plenty of time. Reservations essential. Cancellation fee (30%) will be charged for same-day cancellation. Partially non smoking.

Fukuzushi

5-7-8 Roppongi, Minato-ku; tel: 3402 4116; www.roppongifukuzushi.com; Mon–Sat 11.30am–1.30pm and 6–10pm; station: Roppongi; ¥¥¥¥

Unfailingly good-quality sushi for the well-heeled Roppongi crowd. Expensive, but not snobbish or exclusive. Partially no smoking.

Inakaya East

3-14-7 Roppongi, Minato-ku; tel: 3408 5040; www.roppongiinakaya.jp/en/index.html; daily 5–11pm; station: Roppongi; ¥¥¥¥

Chefs in traditional garb grill fish, meat and vegetables to order, then pass them on long wooden paddles across to where you are sitting. It's theatrical and fun, but not cheap.

Kitchen 5

4-2-15 Nishi-azabu, Minato-ku; tel 3409-8835; http://magazine.kitchen5.jp; Tue, Wed, Fri, and Sat 6–9.30pm; station: Hiroo; ¥¥¥¥

International original cuisine crafted by Yuko Kobayashi. The restaurant closes every summer as Yuko travels the world to explore new recipe horizons. Cash only. No smoking.

Soba (buckwheat) noodles

L'Atelier de Joël Robuchon

2F, Roppongi Hills Hillside, 6-10-1 Roppongi, Minato-ku; tel: 5772 7500; www. robuchon.jp/latelier-en; daily noon–2.30pm and 6–9.30pm; station: Roppongi; ¥¥¥

Robuchon's tapas-influenced cuisine blends informal and sophisticated, but need not break the bank. Counter seating looking into the open kitchen. No smoking.

Ninja

1F, Akasaka Tokyu Plaza, 2-14-3 Nagatacho, Chiyoda-ku; tel: 5157 3936; www.ninjaakasaka.com; Mon–Sat 5–10pm, Sun 5–9.45pm; station: Akasaka; ¥¥¥

In this themed restaurant black-clad waiters dressed like ninja spies show you to your private room, then entertain you as you nibble on simple Japanese food. Lots of fun for all the family.

Nodaiwa

1-5-4 Higashi-Azabu, Minato-ku; tel: 3583 7852; www.nodaiwa.co.jp/english.html; Mon–Sat 11am–1.30pm and 5–8pm; station: Kamiyacho; ¥¥¥

Charcoal-grilled fillets of *unagi* (eel) are daubed with a savoury sauce and served with rice. This is one of best places in Tokyo to try this unsung delicacy of Japanese cuisine.

Pintokona

B2F, Metrohat, 6-4-1 Roppongi, Minato-ku; tel: 5771 1133; daily 11am–10pm; station: Roppongi; ¥¥¥

A stylish conveyor belt sushi restaurant that stresses quality over quantity.

Besides sushi, they also serve a range of light cooked dishes. No smoking.

Tofuya Ukai

4-4-13 Shiba Koen, Minato-ku; tel: 3436 1028; www.ukai.co.jp/english/shiba/index.html; daily 11am–8pm; station: Akabanebashi; ¥¥¥¥

Right below Tokyo Tower, this remarkable restaurant boasts traditional architecture and a beautiful rambling garden with carp ponds. Refined multi-course meals based around tofu are served in private rooms; fully vegetarian food is available by request. No smoking except for bar area.

Aoyama and Harajuku

Benoit

10F La Port Aoyama, 5-51-8 Jingumae, Shibuya-ku; tel: 6419 4181; www.benoit-tokyo.com/en; daily 11.30am–2.15pm, 5.30–9.15pm; station: Omotesando; ¥¥¥

Of French master-chef Alain Ducasse's two restaurants in Tokyo, this one is more informal, concentrating on Mediterranean flavours. No smoking.

Crista

1-2-5 Shibuya, Shibuya-ku; tel: 6418 0077; www.tysons.jp/crista/en; Mon–Fri 11.30am–2pm and 6–10pm, Sat 11am–10pm, Sun until 9pm; stations: Shibuya or Omotesando; ¥¥¥¥

One of the best steakhouses in the city, Crista serves 'traditional American cuisine' with a focus on grilled dishes and seafood, accompanied by a huge

Stylish Jap Cho Ok

cellar of Californian wines. Perfect for expense account entertaining. Partially non-smoking.

Jap Cho Ok

B1F Alteka Belte Plaza, 4-1-15 Minami-Aoyama, Minato-ku; tel: 5410 3408; www.zasoya.com; Mon–Sat 5.30pm–midnight, Sun and hols 5.30–10pm; station: Gaienmae; ¥¥

Stylish yet casual, Jap Cho Ok features seafood dishes and even Zen Buddhist vegetarian temple cooking alongside traditional Korean barbecue. Great decor. Partially no smoking.

Nataraj

B1F Sanwa-Aoyama Building, 2-22-19 Minami-Aoyama, Minato-ku; tel: 5474 0510; www.nataraj.co.jp/en/aoyama/E_AoyamaTop.shtml; Mon–Fri 11.30am–3pm, 6–11pm, Sat–Sun 11.30am–11pm; station: Gaienmae; ¥¥

Tokyo's foremost Indian vegetarian restaurant serves grills and curries from the tandoor oven. Spice levels are mild but can be raised. See also locations in Ginza and Ogikubo. No smoking.

Pure Deli & Store

5-10-17 Minami-Aoyama, Minato-ku; tel: 5466 2611; http://eightablish.com/restaurant; Mon–Fri 9am–10.30pm, Sat 8.30am–10.30pm, Sun 8.30am–10pm; station: Omotesando; ¥

All-day café serving light additive-free and (almost) entirely vegan meals and snacks, including ice cream, muffins and sandwiches. No smoking.

Sasagin

1-32-15 Yoyogi-Uehara, Shibuya-ku; tel: 5454 3715; Mon–Sat 5–11pm; station: Yoyogi-uehara; ¥¥¥

A range of premium sake is served with creative modern Japanese cuisine in a casual setting. The master speaks English and will recommend the best brews.

Two Rooms

3-11-7 Kita Aoyama, Minato-ku; tel: 3498 0002; www.tworooms.jp/en; daily 11.30am–2.30pm, 6–10pm (lounge & bar 11.30am–2am); station: Omotesando; ¥¥¥

Impeccably turned out clientele enjoy fashionable fusion cuisine from a veranda overlooking trendy Aoyama. Weekend brunches and evening bar hours are the times to see and be seen. Partially non smoking.

Yoroniku

B1 6-6-22 Minami-Aoyama, Minato-ku; tel: 3498 4629; Mon–Fri 6–11pm, Sat 5–11pm, Sun 5–10pm; ¥¥¥¥

High end, trendy *yakiniku* (Korean BBQ) restaurant where you can enjoy premium melt-in-your mouth wagyu beef as well as tongue and various entrails.

Shibuya and Ebisu

Afuri

1-1-7 Ebisu, Shibuya-ku; tel: 5795 0750; www.afuri.com; daily 11am–5am; station: Ebisu; ¥¥

Very popular ramen joint. Their *yuzu shio* (citrus salt flavor) ramen is hard to resist. *Tsukemen* (dipping noodle)

Open kitchens reveal craftsmen at work

is also their specialty. Cash only. No smoking. There are also locations in Harajuku, Roppongi Hills, Sangenjaya, Azabu-juban, Roppongi Crossing, and Nakameguro.

Chibo

38F Yebisu Garden Place Tower, 4-20-3 Ebisu, Shibuya-ku; tel: 5424 1011; www. chibo.com; Mon–Fri 11.30am–2.30pm and 5–11pm, Sat–Sun 11.30am–11pm; station: Ebisu; ¥¥

Okonomiyaki (savoury pancakes) made on grills set in the table. Fun food and never expensive, plus a brilliant view. No smoking till 5pm.

Ebisu Imaiya Sohonten

1-7-11 Ebisu-Nishi, Shibuya-ku; tel: 5456 0255; Sat–Thu 5pm–1am, Fri 5pm–3am; station: Ebisu; ¥¥

The speciality is delectable free-range chicken, served either as yakitori (charcoal grilled) or in warming hot-pots before you. Spotless and efficient, and everything is explained in English. Service charge ¥480/person.

Katsu Midori

8F Seibu Shibuya, 21-1 Udagawacho, Shibuya-ku; tel: 5728 4282; http:// katumidori.co.jp; daily 11am–9.45pm; station: Shibuya; ¥¥

Reasonably priced and high-quality conveyor belt sushi place serving highend Midori sushi. Very popular – expect to wait for 30 minutes or longer. Bullet train will deliver your sushi when

you order from an iPad at the table. No smoking.

Sorano

4-17 Sakuragaoka-cho, Shibuya-ku; tel: 5728 5191; Mon–Sat 5–11pm, Sun 5–10.30pm; station: Shibuya; ¥¥¥

Simple and affordable tofu cuisine. Highlights are tofu *shumai* dumplings and *yuba* (soya milk 'skin') prepared at the table. English menu.

Sushi Ouchi

2-8-4 Shibuya, Shibuya-ku; tel: 3407 3543; Mon–Sat 11.30am–1.40pm, 5.30–9.30pm; stations: Shibuya and Omotesando; ¥¥¥

Chef Ouchi plays classical music and prefers a dark-wood decor. All-natural ingredients: no farmed seafood and absolutely no MSG or other chemicals.

Shinjuku

Bistro Kri-Kri

3-38-12 Yoyogi, Shibuya-ku; tel: 5388 9376; Tue–Sun 6pm–midnight; station: Sangubashi; ¥¥¥

Service tends to be slow, but this longtime favourite run by a bohemian couple is worth trying. Their hearty dishes are inspired by the Mediterranean and Middle East, and are complimented by a great selection of wine, and a warm and charming décor. Best to call for reservations.

Hayashi Sumiyaki

2-22-5 Kabuki-cho, Shinjuku-ku; tel: 3209 5672; Mon–Sat 5–11.30pm; station:

Shinjuku; ¥¥
Around the sand hearth, dine on charcoal-grilled meat, fish or seasonal vegetables in a rustic setting. Partially no smoking.

Matsuya

1-1-17 Okubo, Shinjuku-ku; tel: 3200 5733; daily 11am–midnight; station: Shin-Okubo; ¥
A long-established restaurant in Tokyo's Little Seoul, where you sit on the floor at low tables. The speciality is fiery meat-laden stews cooked at the table.

New York Grill

52F Park Hyatt Hotel, 3-7-1-2 Nishi-Shinjuku, Shinjuku-ku; tel: 5323 3458; https://restaurants.tokyo.park.hyatt.co.jp; daily 11.30am–2.30pm, 5.30–10pm; stations: Shinjuku, Tochomae; ¥¥¥¥
Power dining with bravado in a sky-view setting in Shinjuku's Park Hyatt Hotel (the setting for the film *Lost in Translation*). Sunday brunch with cocktails at the adjacent New York Bar is an institution for the expat community. No smoking.

Restaurant Le Coupe Chou

1-15-7 Nishi-Shinjuku, Shinjuku-ku; tel: 3348 1610; daily 11.30am–2pm, 5.30–10pm, closed 3rd Mon of month; station: Shinjuku; ¥¥
In Shinjuku's electronics district, this retro French bistro offers a great-value ¥1,500 four-course lunch. Popular with the local office crowd. No smoking.

Robot Restaurant

B2F 1-7-7 Kabukicho, Shinjuku-ku; tel: 3200 5500; www.shinjuku-robot.com; show starts daily from 1pm, 3pm, 5.30pm, 7.30pm, 9.30pm; station: Shinjuku, Shinjuku Sanchome; ¥¥¥¥
Electric robot extravaganza with girlie show. Admission is ¥8,000. The tasteless bento gets poor reviews, with the only other food options snacks like wings and popcorn, but the performances by robots and sexy female dancers is spectacular and, some say, a once-in-a-lifetime experience. Surprisingly they welcome children, although the admission price is the same as that for adults. Advance online reservations and arriving 30 minutes prior to the show is recommended. Partially non-smoking.

Tokyo Sundubu

B1 3-30-11 Shinjuku, Shinjuku-ku; tel: 5367 3830; www.tokyo-sundubu.net; daily 11am–10pm; station: Shinjuku; ¥¥
Bubbling Korean hot pots with silken tofu and your choice of meat or vegetables. You can choose the level of spiciness and soup broth type from salt, Japanese miso, and Korean miso. No smoking.

Zauo

1F Shinjuku Washington Hotel, 3-2-9 Nishi-Shinjuku, Shinjuku-ku; tel: 3343 6622; www.zauo.com/en; Mon–Fri 11.30–2.30pm and 5–10pm, Sat & Sun 11.30am–2.30pm and 4–10pm; station: Shinjuku; ¥¥¥
Fishing-themed fun restaurant. Tables are arranged around a huge fish tank;

A selection of tempura

diners are invited to catch their own dinner. Great fun for the family. (Fishing option is not available during weekday lunchtime). There are also locations in Shibuya, Meguro and more. Service charge ¥380/person.

Shinagawa and Meguro

Garden Restaurant All Day Dining

3F Shinagawa Goose, 3-13-1 Takanawa, Minato-ku; tel: 5447 1151; www.landmark-tokyo.com/restaurant/alldaydining.html; daily 6.30–9.30am, 11.30am–2.30pm and 5.30–11pm; station: Shinagawa; ¥¥

Reasonable lunch buffet in a relaxing hotel garden atmosphere. Great for families. Window side table reservations are recommended; you can enjoy the garden view. Service charge ¥500/person for dinner. No smoking.

Tsubame Grill

4-10-26 Takanawa, Minato-ku; tel: 3441 0121; www.tsubame-grill.co.jp; daily 11.30am–10.30pm; station: Shinagawa; ¥¥

German style hamburger restaurant offering great value and ambience. Conveniently located near the station. Tsubame's Hamburg steak is a must-try. No smoking.

T.Y. Harbor Brewery

2-1-3 Higashi-Shinagawa, Shingawa-ku; tel: 5479 4555; www.tysons.jp/tyharbor/en; Mon–Fri 11.30am–2pm and 5.30–10pm, Sat–Sun Mon–Fri 11.30am–3pm and 5.30–10pm; stations: Tennozu Isle, Shinagawa; ¥¥

Microbrewed ales and high-quality American bar food, in a canalside setting. English menu. No smoking.

Yanaka and Ueno

Bon

1-2-11 Ryusen, Taito-ku; tel: 3872 0375; www.fuchabon.co.jp/english/english.html; Mon–Fri noon–3pm (last orders 1pm) and 5–9pm (last orders 7pm), Sat noon–9pm (last orders 7pm), Sun noon–8pm (last orders 6pm); station: Iriya; ¥¥¥¥

Memorable multi-course *fucha ryori* (Buddhist vegetarian cuisine), featuring exquisitely prepared seasonal foods in a serene setting. Set menu changes with the seasons. Booking essential.

Innsyoutei

4-59 Ueno Park, Taito-ku; tel: 3821 8126; www.innsyoutei.jp/en; daily 11am–11pm; station: Yushima; ¥¥

Beautiful restaurant in an old house, serving three-tiered box lunches and traditional *kaiseki* dinners. Food is served in a tatami room overlooking the lovely garden.

Nezu No Taiyaki

1-23-9 Nezu, Bunkyo-ku; tel: 3823 6277; Mon–Fri 10am–6pm; station: Nezu; ¥

One of the best-known places in Tokyo to pick up *taiyaki*, a cute pancake in the shape of a sea bream, filled with sweetened red bean paste. They close as soon as they run out, and there's often a queue, so go early.

Takoyaki, Japanese octopus balls

Sasanoyuki

2-15-10 Negishi, Taito-ku; tel: 3873 1145;
www.sasanoyuki.com; Tue–Sun 11.30am–
8pm; station: Uguisudani; ¥¥¥

Tokyo's most historic tofu restaurant is simple and relaxed, with reasonable prices. The set courses here can be quite filling.

Ikebukuro and Mejirodai

Malaychan

3-22-6 Nishi-Ikebukuro, Toshima-ku; tel:
5391 7638; www.malaychan.jp; Tue–Sat
11am–2.30pm, 5–11pm, Sun 11am–11pm,
Mon 5–11pm; station: Ikebukuro; ¥¥

Chinese-Malay cuisine such as shark's fin soup and nasi lemak (rice with coconut milk and spicy toppings), with Thai influences. Partially no smoking.

Mawashizushi

1-28-1 Ikebukuro, Toshima-ku; tel: 6914
1185; daily 11am–11pm; station: Ikebukuro;
¥¥

Modern *kaitenzushi* (conveyor belt sushi) restaurant, with convenient iPad ordering and an excellent menu including crab soup, tempura squid, and clam salad, alongside classic sushi rolls.

Nakiryu

2-34-4 Minami-otsuka, Toshima-ku; tel:
6304 1811; Wed–Sun 11.30am–3pm and
6–9pm, Mon noon–3pm; stations: Otsuka
or Mukohara; ¥¥¥

This tiny restaurant was only the second ramen joint in Tokyo to win a coveted Michelin star, with the house speciality being *tantanmen* – a spicy broth of noodles, pickled vegetables, and pork. There are only 10 seats – arrive early, and be prepared to queue.

Saigon

3F, Torikoma Dai-ichi Building, 1-7-10
Higashi-Ikebukuro, Toshima-ku; tel: 3989
0255; Mon–Fri 11.30am–2pm and 5–10pm,
Sat–Sun 11.30am–2.30pm and 4–10pm;
station: Ikebukuro; ¥¥

Serves down-to-earth Vietnamese fare, including spring rolls, hot pancakes with spicy sauce and beef noodle soup. Set lunches for around ¥1,000.

Asakusa and Ryogoku

Ichimon

3-12-6 Asakusa, Taito-ku; tel: 3875 6800;
www.asakusa-ichimon.com; Mon–Fri
6–11pm, Sat–Sun 5–10pm; station:
Asakusa; ¥¥¥

An atmospheric, well-placed old-world restaurant. Offers excellent sake and a good selection of Japanese dishes.

Otafuku

1-6-2 Senzoku, Taito-ku; tel: 3871 2521;
https://otafuku.ne.jp; Apr–Sep Mon–Sat
5–11pm, Sun 5–10pm, Oct–Mar Mon–Sat
5–11pm, noon–2pm, 4–10pm; station:
Iriya; ¥¥

This venerable restaurant serves *oden* – chunky pieces of fishcake and vegetables simmered in stock – and pine-scented sake.

Unagi (eel) on the grill

Tsukiji and Odaiba

Edogin

4-5-1 Tsukiji, Chuo-ku; tel: 3543 4401; Mon–Sat 11am–9.30pm; station: Tsukiji; ¥¥¥

An old-school sushi emporium, cavernous but packed. The portions are generous, and the location near the Toyosu Fish Market ensures they are fresh.

Khazana

5F Decks Tokyo Beach, 1-6-1 Daiba, Minato-ku; tel: 3599 6551; www.odaiba-decks.com/shop/tenant/post-68; daily 11am–10pm; station: Odaiba Kaihin Koen; ¥¥

All-you-can-eat lunches (until 5pm) and good curries, plus outside tables giving views of the Rainbow Bridge. Numerous other Tokyo locations.

Sakura

3F Hotel Nikko Tokyo, 1-9-1 Daiba, Minato-ku; tel: 5500 5580; daily 11.30am–2.30pm and 5.30–9.30pm; station: Daiba; ¥¥¥¥

Elegant Japanese restaurant in the Hilton hotel, harnessing fresh fish from Tokyo Bay and produce from the surrounding countryside to create delicious traditional dishes. The edomae anago (eel) dishes are particularly good.

Kagurazaka, Suidobashi, Ochanomizu, Kanda and Akihabara

Botan

1-15 Kanda-Sudacho, Chiyoda-ku; tel: 3251 0577; Mon–Sat 11.30am–8pm; station: Akihabara; ¥¥¥¥

Old-style wooden restaurant serving sukiyaki casserole with chicken (not the more usual beef) only. The waitresses explain everything. No smoking.

Kanda Yabu Soba

2-10 Kanda-Awajicho, Chiyoda-ku; tel: 3251 0287; www.yabusoba.net; daily 11.30am–7.30pm; stations: Awajicho, Ogawamachi; ¥

Illustrious noodle shop serving Edo-style handmade soba in a classic, tranquil setting. Cash only. No smoking.

Seigetsu

2F Kamuya Building, 6-77-1 Kagurazaka, Shinjuku-ku; tel: 3269 4320; Mon–Fri 4–11pm, Sat, Sun 4–11pm; stations: Kagurazaka, Ushigome-kagurazaka; ¥¥¥

A casual, modern *izakaya* (tavern) serving above-average Japanese food. Great sake list (in English), with brews from all over Japan.

Stefano

6-47 Kagurazaka, Shinjuku-ku; tel: 5228 7515; www.stefano-jp.com; Thu–Mon 11.30am–2pm, 6–10pm, Tue–Wed 6–10pm; station: Kagurazaka; ¥¥¥

Chef Stefano Fastro serves excellent Italian food, specialising in the cuisine of Venice and the northeast. Home-made pasta and gnocchi. Service charge ¥700/person for dinner. No smoking.

NIGHTLIFE

The last-but-certainly-not-least hours in Tokyo's 24-hour day are a time when busy urbanites unwind at the city's fathomless horizon of 'live house' music venues, dance clubs and DJ bars. The only challenge is deciding when and where to go. Live music venues usually start and end early; DJ bars and dance clubs pick up from there until mid-morning at weekends. Tokyo nightlife tends to be a safe and friendly experience; still, the usual caution is advisable. Due to police vigilance over drugs and under-age drinking, many clubs enforce a 20-and-over policy; photo ID is a must.

Concert tickets can be purchased at box offices, ticket agency Pia (found in major department stores) and convenience store Lawson. English-language listings are available in the *Metropolis* and the daily newspapers, as well as Time Out Tokyo (www.timeout.com/tokyo), Tokyo Gig Guide (www.tokyogigguide.com) and iFlyer (www.iflyer.jp/tokyo).

Bars

Aldgate
30-4 Udagawacho, Shiniwasaki Bldg 3F, Shibuya-ku; tel: 3462 2983; daily 6pm–2am; station: Shibuya
One of a few brewpubs in Tokyo to offer both free Wi-Fi and a non-smoking environment. An excellent selection of beer on top is complimented by decent English pub fare, a tasteful rock music selection and friendly international crowd.

Awabar
4-10-11 Roppongi, Minato-ku; tel: 6804 5739; www.awabar.jp; Mon–Fri 6pm–3am, Sat 6pm–midnight; station: Roppongi
Small, buzzy bar with a wide range of beers on tap and, unusually, a similarly extensive menu of champagnes and sparkling wines.

Fiesta International Karaoke Bar
6-2-35 B1 Roppongi 662 Building, Minato-ku; tel: 5410 3008; www.fiesta-roppongi.com; Mon–Sat 7pm–5am; station: Roppongi
A legendary English-language karaoke bar with over 10,000 international hits and 70,000 Japanese songs catering to an international crowd. ¥3,500 entry includes three drinks.

The Footnik
1F Asahi Building, 1-11-2 Ebisu, Shibuya-ku; tel: 5795 0144; www.footnik.net; daily 3pm–1am; station: Ebisu
This British football pub draws expats and Japanese football fans alike with big-screen TVs. There's another branch in Osaki (1F ThinkPark, 2-1-1 Osaki, Shinagawa-ku; tel: 5759 1044).

New York Bar

52F Park Hyatt Hotel, 3-7-1-2 Nishi Shinjuku, Shinjuku-ku; tel: 5323 3458; http://tokyo.park.hyatt.com; daily 5pm–midnight, Thu–Sat until 1am; station: Tochomae

Located on the upper floors of the luxurious Park Hyatt Hotel, this spot is popular because of its night views over Tokyo. The drinks list is impressive and the service impeccable. There's a ¥2,500 cover charge from 8pm (7pm on Sun) for non-guests.

Old Imperial Bar

Imperial Hotel, 1-1-1 Uchisaiwai-cho, Hibiya, Chiyoda-ku; tel: 3539 8088; www. imperialhotel.co.jp; daily 11.30am–midnight; station: Hibiya

The hotel's legendary bar is the only part of it that preserves the original Frank Lloyd Wright Art Deco design from the 1920s. Order their original Mount Fuji cocktail.

The Pink Cow

B1 Bright Building, 2-7-5 Minato-ku, Akasaka; tel: 6441 2998; www.thepinkcow. com; Mon–Fri 11.30am–3pm, 6pm–late, Sat 6pm–late; station: Akasaka

Loved by the art, fashion and media crowd, this café-bar offers a good range of wine, beers and cocktails as well as food. Events include poetry readings, jazz concerts, book launches and art exhibitions.

Sekirei

Meiji Kinenkan, 2-2-23 Moto-Akasaka, Minato-ku; tel: 3746 7723; www. meijikinenkan.gr.jp; July–mid-Sep Mon–Fri 5–10pm; station: Shinanomachi

At this elegant summer-only bar, inside the grand Meiji Kinenkan wedding and party hall, look out on a garden where classical Japanese dance is performed nightly.

Gay venues

Most of Shinjuku Ni-chome's 300 or more hole-in-the-wall gay clubs and bars generally do not welcome casual visitors or foreigners who do not speak Japanese. The listed venues are both welcoming to all comers and relatively easy to find.

Arty Farty

2-11-7 Shinjuku, Shinjuku-ku; tel: 5362 9720; www.arty-farty.net; Sun–Thu 8pm–4am, Fri–Sat 8pm–5am; station: Shinjuku-Sanchome

Gay dance bar with a mostly male clientele, although an exception is made on Sundays when women accompanied by gay male friends are allowed in.

GB

B1F, Business Shinjuku Plaza Building, 2-12-3 Shinjuku, Shinjuku-ku; tel: 3352 8972; www.gb-tokyo.com; Mon–Thu 8pm–2am, Fri–Sat until 3am, Sun 7pm–midnight; station: Shinjuku-Sanchome

A men-only venue that is one of the favourite spots in Tokyo for meetings between foreigners and locals.

Choosing a drink in a Roppongi bar

Leo Lounge

2-14-16 Shinjuku, Shinjuku-ku; tel:
5341 4380; www.leolounge.jp; Sun–Thu
noon–5am, Fri–Sat 6pm–5am; station:
Shinjuku-Sanchome

One of the most popular gay bars in the
city, with a friendly atmosphere, karaoke, and regular cabaret and drag performances.

Live jazz

Billboard Live

4F Tokyo Midtown, 9-7-4 Akasaka, Minato-
ku; tel: 3405 1133; www.billboard-live.
com; shows daily 6.30 and 9.30pm; station:
Roppongi

Licensed by the American music industry trade magazine *Billboard*, this glistening international jazz and pop
supper club is a centrepiece of Roppongi's Tokyo Midtown development.

Blue Note Tokyo

6-3-16 Minami-Aoyama, Minato-ku; tel:
5485 0088; www.bluenote.co.jp; station:
Omotesando

Top international acts appear in this
sophisticated venue. The ambience is
much like that of the original venue in
the US.

Pit Inn

B1F Accord Building, 2-12-4
Shinjuku, Shinjuku-ku; tel: 3354 2024;
www.pit-inn.com; station: Shinjuku-
Sanchome

For over 40 years, Pit Inn has been a
temple of jazz for the Tokyo faithful,
featuring avant-garde innovators like
Yoshihide Otomo and the occasional
overseas act. Evening entry tends to run
to ¥3,000 including one drink.

Live popular music

Club Asia

1-8 Maruyama-cho, Shibuya-ku; tel: 5458
2551; www.clubasia.co.jp; station: Shibuya

The dance floors and bars on different
levels are an interesting design feature,
although the music can get warped in
the process. Typical of Tokyo's multi-use
spaces, Club Asia might host a punk
band in the evening, followed by a night
of club jazz, trance or dancehall.

Club Quattro

5F Parco Quattro, 32-13 Udagawacho,
Shibuya-ku; tel: 3477 8750; www.club-
quattro.com; Shibuya

International rock and world music
bands as well as local groups play at
this intimate venue, which is one of
Tokyo's most storied stages.

Crocodile

B1, 6-18-8 Jingumae, Shibuya-ku; tel:
3499 5205; http://crocodile-live.jp; daily
6pm–1am; station: Shibuya

One of the oldest live-music venues in
Tokyo, Crocodile has expanded its rep-
ertoire over the years to include not
just rock, but whatever happens to be
hip, including rap bands, Latin combos
and jazz. Also hosts English shows by
the Tokyo Comedy Store's Improvazilla
(www.improvazilla.com).

David Roberts performing at Club Quattro

Liquidroom

3-16-6 Higashi, Shibuya-ku; tel: 5464 0800; www.liquidroom.net; station: Roppongi

Replacing the former Liquidroom in Shinjuku, this iconic club has rebranded to be more of a live music space than an electronic venue, with bands and artists performing daytime and evening gigs, although later events with DJs are occasionally hosted too. There's room for about 900 people, and it regularly sells out, so book ahead.

Unit

1-34-17 Ebisu-nishi, Za House Bldg, Meguro-ku; tel: 5459 8630; http://unit-tokyo.com; station: Ebisu

This three-storey underground complex does it all: live music concerts by leading domestic and international acts, and dance music all-nighters on weekends.

Dance clubs

Ageha

2-2-10 Shin-Kiba, Koto-ku; tel: 5534 2525; www.ageha-en.com; Fri–Sat 11pm–late; station: Shin-Kiba

Tokyo's biggest dance club, with three separate dance rooms and a poolside bar. Hundreds of clubbers bus in from Shibuya for massive hip-hop, house, techno and trance EDM parties.

Contact

B2F Shintaiso Building, 2-10-2 Dogenzaka, Shibuya-ku; tel: 6427 8107; www.contacttokyo.com; Mon–Wed 9pm–late, Fri–Sat 10pm–late; station: Shibuya

Since the closure of the legendary Air, the trendy Contact has assumed the mantle of the place to go for Tokyoites in the know when it comes to electronic music. With carefully curated line-ups and one of the best soundsystems in the city, this is one for the purists.

ELE Tokyo

Warehouse 702, B1F Fukao Building, 1-4-5 Azabu-juban, Minato-ku; tel: 5572 7535; http://eletokyo.com; Thu–Sat 10pm–late; station: Azabu-juban

One of Tokyo's larger clubs, this long, narrow underground space with a stage at one end and a bar at the other promises the latest EDM sounds and fashions.

Sound Museum Vision

2-10-7 Dogenzaka, Shintaiso Bldg. B1F; Shibuya-ku; tel: 5728-2824; www.vision-tokyo.com; Fri–Sat 10pm–late; station: Shibuya

This vast warren of rooms beneath Shibuya is a labyrinth of dance floors, bars and chill-out spaces. Run by one of Tokyo's most experienced promoters, the bills take in a wide range of house, techno, EDM, hip-hop and diverse forms of dance music.

Womb

2-16 Maruyama-cho, Shibuya-ku; tel: 5459 0039; www.womb.co.jp; Mon–Thu 10pm–late, Fri–Sat 11pm–late, Sun 4–10pm; station: Shibuya

This cavernous four-floor club is one of the serious dance-culture venues in Tokyo. What it lacks in atmosphere it makes up for with excellent music and a gargantuan sound system.

A–Z

A

Addresses

Tokyo is divided into 23 *ku* (wards), which are subdivided into *cho* (districts), then numbered *chome* (blocks). Addresses in Japanese start with the city (outside of Tokyo it would be the *ken* or prefecture), followed by ward name, then district, city block and building numbers. For example, the address of the Tokyo Metropolitan Government Building would be written: Tokyo, Shinjuku-ku, Nishi-Shinjuku 2-8-1. This order is reversed when written in roman letters (the order used in this guide).

When navigating the city, Japanese people think in terms of city blocks, often finding their way from one to the next using landmarks. Even taxi drivers get confused away from the main thoroughfares.

B

Budgeting

Tokyo need not be as expensive as you might fear. Staying at a hostel and eating cheaply can be done on a budget of ¥5,000 a day, although ¥10,000–15,000 is more reasonable. While five-star hotels can start from around ¥20,000 a night, there are plenty of mid-range options available for ¥8,000–15,000, sometimes with a light breakfast included. Lunchtime set-meal bargains can run to ¥1,000–2,000, and there are lots of inexpensive options such as noodle bars and revolving sushi restaurants. Drinking alcohol, though, can boost the bill substantially; the cheapest beer is typically around ¥700 a glass. Public transport is inexpensive, and entry to most attractions is reasonable.

The **GRUTT Pass** is a ¥2,200 ticket covering entry to 66 public, national and private institutions, including all Tokyo's major museums. It is valid for two months after first being used, and can be bought at participating venues and the Tokyo Tourist Information Centre in the Tokyo Metropolitan Government Building, Shinjuku.

C

Children

Although Tokyo is short on public parks and playgrounds, the city is like a giant hi-tech theme park in which kids are rollercoastered about on futuristic trains and monorails, greeted by flashing screens at every turn. Tokyo's safety, its abundant and clean public toilets, and its many pharmacies for infant necessities also make it a good choice for families.

For further English resources see www.tokyowithkids.com, an 'interactive online community for English-speaking parents in Tokyo'. Note that some of the information here can be out of date.

Asakusa Senso-Ji Pagoda and Main Temple

Clothing

Tokyoites are both highly fashionable and often quite formal in what they wear. Depending on the social occasion you might feel out of place if you dress too casually. Large *gaijin* (foreigners) will find it difficult to buy large-size clothes and shoes – for women this may even apply to anyone above petite. Slip-on shoes are best, as they will need to be removed on entering homes and some restaurants and other places.

Crime and safety

Tokyo is one of the safest cities in the world, but visitors shouldn't become too nonchalant. Although rare, pickpocketing and muggings do happen, as do worse crimes. Police boxes (*koban*) can be found in all neighbourhoods, often near the major train stations.

Customs

Non-residents entering the country are given a duty-free allowance of 400 cigarettes, 100 cigars, 500g of tobacco, three 760ml bottles of alcohol, 2oz of perfume and gifts the total value of which is less than ¥200,000. For more information, see www.customs.go.jp.

D

Disabled travellers

While there is a drive to provide more accessible hotels, tourist facilities and public transport for disabled travellers, Tokyo is not an easy place for limited-mobility people to get around. Useful, but outdated, information is available at http://accessible.jp.org.

E

Earthquakes

Tokyo is notoriously susceptible to earthquakes. It is wise, therefore, to check the emergency exits in your hotel. In the event of a tremor, safety precautions include turning off any electrical or gas sources, opening exits, and standing or crouching under a sturdy door lintel or heavy table.

Electricity

The current in Tokyo is 100 volts AC, 50 cycles. American-style plugs with two flat pins are used. Adaptors and transformers are required if you come from countries like Britain where the voltage is 240.

Embassies

Australia: 2-1-14 Mita, Minato-ku; tel: 5232 4111; http://japan.embassy.gov.au

Canada: 7-3-38 Akasaka, Minato-ku; tel: 5412 6200; www.canadainternational.gc.ca/japan-japon

UK: 1 Ichiban-cho, Chiyoda-ku; tel: 5211 1100; http://ukinjapan.fco.gov.uk

US: 1-10-5 Akasaka, Minato-ku; tel: 3224 5000; http://jp.usembassy.gov

Taking in the view from the Mori Tower at Roppongi Hills

Emergency numbers

Ambulance and Fire: 119; Police: 110; Japan Helpline: 0120-461 997.

Etiquette

While allowances are made for unschooled foreigners, a few pointers are useful, as some behaviour can cause genuine offence or embarrassment.

Always remove your shoes before entering Japanese homes, inns and certain museums and restaurants. Rows of slippers at entrances indicate their use. Shoeboxes or lockers are other hints. Remove slippers before stepping onto *tatami* (woven straw) mats. You will also be required to switch slippers to a separate pair before entering a toilet.

Blowing one's nose in public is a gross faux pas.

When someone pours you a drink, you are expected to lift your glass slightly off the table and then pour the other person's drink.

Chopsticks are never left sticking in rice, a gesture associated with the dead.

Eating on the train or while walking the street is viewed as poor manners.

G

Green issues

With one of the world's best public transport networks, there are few places in Tokyo that are solely accessible by using a car or taxi. Separation and some recycling of trash is practised; you will find separate waste bins for burnable and non-burnable rubbish as well as cans, bottles and paper. Carry your own pair of chopsticks rather than using the disposable ones provided at almost every restaurant.

H

Health and medical care

No vaccinations are required to enter Japan. Tap water is safe, and medical care is good. Hospitals and clinics with English-speaking staff include:

Japanese Red Cross Medical Centre, 4-1-22 Hiro-o, Shibuya-ku; tel: 3400 1311; www.med.jrc.or.jp

Jikei University Hospital, 3-19-1 Nishishinbashi, Minato-ku; tel: 3433 1111; www.jikei.ac.jp

St Luke's International Hospital, 9-1 Akashicho, Chuo-ku; tel: 5550 7120; http://hospital.luke.ac.jp

Tokyo Medical and Surgical Clinic, 2F 32 Shiba-koen Building, 3-4-30 Shiba-koen, Minato-ku; tel: 3436 3028; www.tmsc.jp

Hours and holidays

Officially business hours are Mon–Fri 9am–5pm, but office workers often stay later. Shops open through the week, usually from around 10am to 7 or 8pm; many are open Sundays and closed another day of the week. Most restaurants open at around 11.30am and take last orders at about 9.30pm.

Kenzo Tange's Fuji TV Building, Odaiba

Museums often close on Mondays. Restaurants, department stores and museums usually open on public holidays.

Public holidays
1 Jan: New Year's Day
2nd Mon Jan: Coming of Age Day
11 Feb: Foundation Day
23 Feb: Emperor's Birthday
20–1 Mar: Spring Equinox
29 Apr: Green Day
3 May: Constitution Memorial Day
4 May: National Holiday
5 May: Children's Day
3rd Mon July: Marine Day
11 August: Mountain Day
3rd Mon Sept: Respect the Aged Day
23–4 Sept: Autumn Equinox
2nd Mon Oct: Sports Day
3 Nov: Culture Day
23 Nov: Labour Day

I

Internet

The internet can be accessed in most hotel rooms as well as airbnb accommodations, either via LAN cable or Wi-Fi. Internet cafés can be found across the city, usually as part of 24-hour computer game and manga centres. Free Wi-Fi spots are increasing but still scarce compared to many western cities. See Tokyo Metro (www.tokyometro.jp/en/tips/connectivity/freewifi) and NTT's Japan Connected-free Wi-Fi (www.ntt-bp.net/jcfw/en.html) and tourist-only Free Wi-Fi Japan (http://flets.com/freewifi/spot.

html) for registration details on free public Wi-Fi systems. Yet another option is to rent a mobile Wi-Fi router at Narita (www.narita-airport.jp/en/guide/service/list/svc_19.html) or Haneda airports (www.haneda-airport.jp/inter/en/premises/service/internet.html).

L

Language

With its three alphabets, Japanese is a notoriously difficult language to learn. However, don't let this put you off trying to master a few simple words and phrases. As a spoken language, Japanese is relatively easy to pronounce, and when used even in a basic form will often be greeted by the locals with joy. English is not widely spoken, but many people will understand written English, and it can be useful to write down what you're trying to communicate. For some basic phrases, see page 134.

LGBTQ travellers

Homosexuals tend to keep a low profile in Japan, and do not promote themselves in Tokyo as much as they do in other international cities. However, Tokyo is fairly tolerant of gay and alternative lifestyles, and has a thriving scene with a selection of clubs, events and support networks. It is mainly centred around Shinjuku in an area called Ni-chome, near to Shinjuku-Sanchome Station. Most of the bars, clubs and saunas here cater to the local gay

community, but there are a number of places for non-Japanese-speakers.

A useful online starting point is Travel Gay Asia (www.travelgayasia.com/tokyo-gay-bars).

Lost property

Chances are if you lose something in Tokyo, you will get it back. The train and subway systems both have highly efficient lost-property offices, as do many public buildings. Also check with the local police boxes (koban), found in all neighbourhoods.

Maps

Tourist offices provide adequate maps of the city for free. For more detail, buy the indispensable *Tokyo City Atlas: A Bilingual Guide*, published by Kondansha. Google Maps also now includes comprehensive views and information on Tokyo.

Media

Newspapers and magazines. Daily papers available in English include the *Japan Times* (www.japantimes.co.jp), packaged with *The New York Times*, and *The Japan News* (http://the-japan-news.com). Tokyo has several English-language listings magazines that can be picked up at the airport, in large English bookshops and hotels. The best is the free biweekly *Metropolis* (http://metropolisjapan.com). Also worth a look are *Time Out Tokyo* (www.time-

out.com/tokyo) and *Tokyo Weekender* (www.tokyoweekender.com).

Television and radio. State broadcaster NHK offers NHK on channel 1, NHK Educational on channel 3 and the new NHK World channel (www.nhk.or.jp/nhk-world). The other main Tokyo channels are Nihon TV (channel 4), TBS (6), Fuji TV (8), TV Asahi (10) and TV Tokyo (12).

Radio Japan (www.nhk.or.jp/nhk-world) offers programmes in 18 different languages. Inter FM (76.1MHz; www.interfm.co.jp) has some English-language news, and you can also hear a small amount of English programming on J-WAVE (81.3MHz).

Money

The Japanese yen (¥) is available in 1-, 5-, 10-, 50-, 100- and 500-yen coins and 1,000, 2,000, 5,000 and 10,000 notes. Money can be exchanged at banks and authorised exchangers. Many shops do not accept credit cards, so carry a reasonable amount of cash. Major credit cards and cash cards linked to Cirrus, PLUS, Maestro and Visa Electron networks can be used at post office and Seven Bank (located at 7-Eleven stores) ATMs. Traveller's cheques are accepted by leading banks, hotels and stores.

Police

You can dial the police number (110) from any public phone, free of charge. Chances are, you won't have to walk

Japanese currency

more than a few blocks to find a local police box *(koban)*.

Post

Post offices are open Mon–Fri 9am–5pm; some are also open Sat 9am–3pm. For English-language information about postal services, including postal fees, call 0570-046 111 or go to www.post.japan post.jp. Tokyo Central Post Office (2-7-2 Marunouchi, Chiyoda-ku; tel: 3284 9539) is open Mon–Fri 9am–9pm, Sat– Sun 9am–7pm. The Tokyo International Post Office (3-5-1 Shinsuna, Koto-ku), is open daily 24 hours.

R

Religion

Shinto is Japan's indigenous religion, an animist faith that involves the worship of spirits, or *kami*. Shinto shrines (indicated by the suffix *-jinja, -jingu* or *-gu*) are generally un-flamboyant in design, the most notable feature being the simple wooden *torii* gate, which symbolises a door between the earthly realm and that of the *kami*. In contrast, Buddhist temples (*-tera, -dera, -ji* or *-in*), such as Asakusa's Senso-ji, are more extravagant, with imposing entry gates flanked by fearsome statues of celestial guardians, or *Nio*.

T

Telephones

Phone numbers. Tokyo's area code is 03, but you don't need to dial this within the city. All regular telephone numbers have eight digits. Other area codes are Hakone: 0460, Kamakura: 0467, Kawagoe: 0492, Narita: 0476 and Nikko: 0288.

Local numbers beginning with 0120, 0088 or 0053 are toll-free calls that can be dialled only within Japan.

If calling from one province to another, dial the area code first (with the zero).

International calls. To dial Tokyo from the UK dial 00 (international code) + 81 (Japan) + area code (minus the initial 0) + the number. To call overseas from Tokyo, dial the access code of an international call-service provider (KDDI: 001, Japan Telecom: 0041, NTT: 0033, Cable & Wireless IDC: 0061), then the country code and the number.

For directory assistance.
NTT Information Service – tel: 0120-505 506. In English.
Local directory assistance – tel: 104. Ask for an English-speaking operator.
International directory assistance (English-speaking) – tel: 0051.

Public telephones. Public telephones take telephone cards, although some may accept ¥10 and ¥100 coins. Each carrier issues its own prepaid cards: NTT and DDI (domestic) and KDD (international). The cards can only be used at the appropriate telephone booth.

Mobile/cell phones. NTT DoCoMo (www.nttdocomo.co.jp) and SoftBank Mobile (www.softbank-rental.jp) allow visitors to use their own numbers

5 Yamanote Line
東京・目黒方面
for Tōkyō & Meguro

4 Keihin-Tōhoku Line
東京・横浜方面
for Tōkyō & Yokohama

Station signage is also handily in English

and SIM cards with their 4G services, although you will need to rent or buy a phone in Japan. Alternatively, rent a phone or a SIM card with a Japan-based number at Narita and Haneda Airports to use during your stay. Most mobile numbers begin with 090 or 080.

Time zones

Tokyo (like the rest of Japan) is +9 hours GMT, +14 hours EST (New York) and +17 PST (Los Angeles). Japan does not have summer daylight-saving time.

Tipping

Tipping is not practised in Japan. However, some restaurants do impose a 10 percent service charge.

Tourist information

Japan National Tourist Organisation (JNTO; 2-10-1 Yurakucho, Chiyoda-ku; tel: 3216 1903; www.jnto.go.jp; Mon–Fri 9am–5pm, Sat 9am–noon) offers information on all of Japan as well as Tokyo. For city-specific details, visit the **Tokyo Tourist Information Centre** (1F Tokyo Metropolitan Government No. 1 Building, 2-8-1 Nishi-Shinjuku; tel: 5321 3077; daily 9.30am–6.30pm), also at **Haneda Airport** (tel: 6428 0653; daily 24 hours) and in the Kesei line station at Ueno (tel: 3836 3471; daily 8am–6.30pm).

The websites of the **Tokyo Convention and Visitors Bureau** (www.tcvb. or.jp) and **Visit Tokyo** (www.gotokyo.org) have up-to-date information.

Transport

Arrival by air

New Tokyo International Airport (Narita; tel: 0476-348 000; www.narita-airport.jp) is about 66km (40 miles) east of the city, and **Tokyo International Airport** (Haneda; tel: 5757 8111; www.haneda-airport.jp) is 15km (10 miles) to the south. The city's two airports are usually referred to as Narita and Haneda. Most international flights arrive at Narita, but with the opening of a new runway, Haneda will see more flights to neighbouring countries.

Four big airlines serve Tokyo from the UK: British Airways, JAL, ANA and Virgin Atlantic. From the US or Canada, JAL and ANA, Northwest, American Airlines, Delta, Continental and United Airlines all have routes. Tokyo is also an increasingly important hub for flights to Asian destinations.

April, August and December tend to be the most expensive times to fly to Japan, as they coincide with the country's Golden Week, O-bon and Christmas-New Year holidays. Flying a few days either side of these peak periods can result in huge savings.

Narita Airport to the city

Taxi. This is the most expensive option and usually the slowest. The fare to Tokyo is ¥20,000–30,000, but it's no quicker than the bus.

Limousine bus. Frequent and comfortable airport limousine buses (tel:

A famous bullet train

3665 7220; www.limousinebus.co.jp) are much cheaper than taxis; they cost ¥3,100 to most central Tokyo locations. The buses connect Narita Airport with most parts of the city, including major hotels, railway stations and Tokyo City Air Terminal (a pre-boarding check-in facility), as well as Haneda Airport and Tokyo Disneyland. Tickets can be bought in the arrivals lobby after clearing immigration and customs. Buses are boarded outside the terminal.

Train. This is the fastest way to reach Tokyo. Stations for the two competing express services are found on the basement level of both terminal buildings.

The **JR Narita Express** (tel: 2016 1603; www.jreast.co.jp/e/nex) connects with the JR railway network at Tokyo, Shinagawa, Shinjuku, Ikebukuro, Omiya, Yokohama and Ofuna stations. It takes an hour to Tokyo Station and the price is ¥3,020 for standard class.

The **Keisei Skyliner** (www.keisei.co.jp) runs to Tokyo's Ueno Station, stopping first at Nippori. The connection to JR lines or the subway at Ueno is not as convenient as the Narita Express, but the Skyliner is usually less crowded. It takes an hour to Ueno, costing ¥2,470.

Both the JR and Keisei lines offer cheaper but slower non-express train services to the city.

Haneda Airport to the city

Taxi. It should take about 30 minutes to central Tokyo by taxi, costing around ¥5,000–8,000; but beware of traffic congestion.

Train. Most people opt for the cheaper trains. Frequent services run from the Keihin Kyuko Station in the airport basement. The train takes about 20 minutes to Shinagawa Station and costs ¥400.

Monorail. The Tokyo Monorail connects Haneda with Hamamatsucho Station on the JR Yamanote line. It takes only 17 minutes and costs ¥410, but can be very crowded.

Limousine bus. An airport limousine bus service connects Haneda with central Tokyo. Fares start at ¥1,000, depending on which part of the city you are heading to. There is also a service from Haneda to Narita that takes about 75 minutes and costs ¥3,100.

Arrival by road

Expressways are of extraordinarily high quality. Like in Britain, the Japanese drive on the left. Highway tolls are high, making trains and buses generally more economical.

Japan has an excellent system of **inter-city buses**. They are a comfortable and cheaper alternative to the bullet train. Buses include destinations not covered by trains, and many services are direct. Night buses are the cheapest, but leave late and arrive early. Some of these are operated by Japan Railways; buy tickets at the Green Window offices at JR stations.

Tokyo taxi

The main JR bus office, where services from Kyoto and Osaka arrive, is on the Yaesu (east) side of Tokyo Station.

Arrival by train

The majority of train lines entering Tokyo from major Japanese cities, whether regular or Shinkansen (bullet train), stop at Tokyo Station on the JR Yamanote line. Day trips to places like Hakone usually involve taking a private (non-JR) line. Most of these connect with major JR terminals like Shibuya and Shinjuku stations.

Transportation within Tokyo

Subway. Tokyo's clean, safe and convenient subway – made up of the nine-line **Tokyo Metro** (www.tokyometro.jp) and the four-line **Toei** (www.kotsu.metro.tokyo.jp) – is the fastest and most economical means of getting across town.

The two systems are fully integrated and run to precise schedules indicated on timetables posted at each station. Services run from 5am to 12.30am at intervals of 2–3 minutes during rush hours, with frequencies dropping to around every 5–10 minutes in off-peak periods. The frequency reduces slightly at weekends. All stations have a route map indicating fares for each stop near the ticket machines, usually in English.

Fares are regulated on a station-to-station basis, so if you cannot determine the fare required, just purchase the cheapest ticket available

(¥170 for Tokyo Metro lines, ¥180 for Toei lines) at the ticket machine. Fare correction can be done on arrival.

Pasmo magnetic smart cards (www.pasmo.co.jp), good on any public transport line in Tokyo, can be bought at subway stations (¥500 deposit) and recharged when depleted. These are simply passed over sensors of the automated ticket gates as you enter, with the fare deducted at your destination. JR's Suica cards act in exactly the same way, and both can be used on subways, trains and buses.

Trains. Above ground, **Japan Railways** (JR) operate a service as efficient as the subway, with equivalent frequency and operating hours (5am–1am) on commuter lines. Like the subways, the lines are colour-coded.

The Yamanote line (green) makes a 35km (20-mile) oval loop around central Tokyo, with JR and private lines branching out to the suburbs. Also useful is the Chuo line (orange) that runs east–west, connecting Tokyo Station with Shinjuku Station and beyond. JR fares start at ¥140. Prepaid, chargeable Suica cards can be used instead of cash at ticket machines. A one-day Tokunai Pass (¥750) is good for unlimited JR train travel in central Tokyo.

Buses. There are no English signs on Tokyo buses, but imminent stops are announced by a recorded voice. Passengers pay on entry, dropping the flat fare (¥200) into a box located next to

the driver; there's a machine in the box for changing notes if you don't have the coins. Tourist information centres and hotels can give you bus maps with the major routes marked. Buses generally run 5.30am–midnight.

Ferry. Tokyo River Buses (tel: 5733 4812; www.suijobus.co.jp) offer a range of services down the Sumida River and across Tokyo Bay. For details of their most popular route, connecting Asakusa and Hama Rikyu Garden, see page . Other routes include a cruise around Tokyo Harbour (45 min), past Rainbow Bridge to Kasai Sealife Park (55 min), and to the Shinagawa Aquarium (35 min). All boats depart from Hinode Pier, near Takeshiba Station on the Yurikamome line. Look out for the striking, sci-fi-esque *Himiko* vessel, designed by *manga* artist Leiji Matsumoto, which morphs into the floating bar Jicoo at night (www.jicoofloatingbar.com).

Taxis. Taxis are a convenient but pricey way of getting around. The standard flagfall in Tokyo is ¥430; anything other than short trips can run from ¥3,000 to ¥5,000. No tipping is expected.

Taxis are readily available on the streets, and at every major hotel and railway station. A red light in the front window signifies that the taxi is available. Roads are narrow and traffic congestion is appalling at rush hour.

Most taxi drivers speak only Japanese, so it helps to have your destination written down in Japanese. Do not

be surprised if taxis fail to stop when you hail them, particularly at night. Drivers will be looking for profitable runs to the suburbs rather than foreigners wanting to return to their hotels.

Note that there is no need to touch the door when getting in or out of taxi – they are automatically opened and closed by the driver.

Recommended taxi operators are:

Nihon Kotsu: tel: 5755 2151; www. nihon-kotsu.co.jp

Tokyo Taxi: tel: 3212 0505; www.tokyo-taxi.jp

Driving and car rental. Tokyo is not an easy place in which to drive. Except on the often crowded expressways, there are few road signs in romanised Japanese, and parking is always a problem. For getting out of town, it is usually faster to take public transport. If you do need to hire a car, try **Toyota Rent-a-Car** (http://rent.toyota.co.jp), which has branches at the airports and across the city.

V

Visas

Nationals of most Western countries do not need a visa for a short visit. On arrival, visitors are usually granted temporary visitor status, good for 90 days. Anyone wishing to extend their stay should visit the Tokyo Regional Immigration Bureau office (5-5-30 Konan, Minato-ku; tel: 5796 7111; www.moj. go.jp).

LANGUAGE

With its three alphabets, Japanese is notoriously difficult. However, don't let this put you off trying to master a few words. As a spoken language, Japanese is simple, and when used will often be greeted by locals with joy. Japan is pouring billions of dollars into English ahead of the 2020 Olympics, but Japanese is still spoken almost exclusively. Signs are generally written with Roman letters, increasingly with English, Chinese and Korean translations.

Excellent translation tools now exist online, in the form of Google Translate and other applications such as the browser add-on Rikaichan. A superior Japanese translation app for the phone is imiwa? for iOS. Equipping yourself with one or all of these will expand your communication potential immensely.

Japanese uses three different forms of writing: two homegrown phonetic scripts hiragana and katakana, each of which consists of 46 basic characters; plus Chinese characters (kanji). The most important words to remember are the simple kanji for 'man' and 'woman'—useful at hot-spring resorts and public toilets.

With its small number of simple and unvarying vowel sounds, the pronunciation of Japanese should be easy for those who speak Western languages, which are rich in vowel sounds, and Japanese has nothing like the tonal system of Chinese.

Vowels have only one sound. Don't be sloppy with their pronunciations.

a – between fat and the u in but
e – like the e in egg
i – like the i in ink
o – like the o in orange
u – like the u in butcher

When they occur in the middle of words between voiceless consonants (ch, f, h, k, p, s, sh, t and ts), i and u are often almost silent. For example, *Takeshita* is really pronounced *Takesh'ta* while *sukiyaki* sounds more like *s'kiyaki*.

Useful words and phrases

Hello *Konnichiwa*
Goodbye *Sayonara*
Please *Onegaishimasu*
Thank you *Domo arigato*
Yes *Hai*
No *Iie*
Excuse me *Sumimasen*
I'm sorry *Gomennasai*
Do you speak English? *Eigo o hanasemasuka?*
I don't understand *Wakarimasen*
Help! *Tasukete!*
My name is … *Watashi wa … desu*
What is your name? *Anata no namae wa nan desu ka?*
Where is the toilet? *Toire wa doko desu ka?*
Woman *Onna*
Man *Otoko*
Child *Kodomo*

Japanese characters are hard to read but beautiful to look at

Getting around

Where is the ...? *... wa doko desu ka?*

What time is it? *Nanji desu ka?*

What time is the...? *...wa nanji desu ka?*

Airport *Kuukou*

Station *Eki*

Bank *Ginko*

Eating out

Food *Tabemono*

Drink *Nomimono*

Water *Omizu*

How much does this cost? *Ikura desu ka?*

Is there an English menu? *Eigo no menyu wa arimasu ka?*

Delicious *Oishi*

The bill, please

Okanjo *kudasai*

Thank you for the meal *Gochiso sama deshita*

Rice *gohan* (cooked), *kome* (raw)

Noodles *Men*

Bread *Pan*

Fish *Sakana*

Beef *Gyuniku*

Pork *Butaniku*

Chicken *Toriniku*

Vegetables *Yasai*

Water *Omizu*

Black Tea *Kocha*

Green Tea *Ocha*

Coffee *Kohi*

Sukiyaki **Simmered meat (usually beef) hotpot, served with raw egg**

Shabushabu **Thinly sliced meat (usually beef) and vegetable hotpot, served with sauce**

Gyudon **Beef on rice**

Kare **curry, but much sweeter**

Tempura **Batter-fried seafood and vegetables**

Teppanyaki **Grilled food**

Tonkatsu **Breaded, deep-fried pork**

Yakosoba **Fried noodles**

Numbers

1 *ichi*

2 *ni*

3 *san*

4 *shi*

5 *go*

6 *roku*

7 *nana*

8 *hachi*

9 *kyu*

10 *ju*

Days of the week

Monday *Getsuyoubi*

Tuesday *Kayoubi*

Wednesday *Suiyoubi*

Thursday *Mokuyoubi*

Friday *Kinyoubi*

Saturday *Doyoubi*

Sunday *Nichiyobi*

Technology

Internet *Intahnetto*

Wi-Fi *Waifai*

Mobile phone *Kaytai Denwa*

Computer *Konpyuhtah*

Electricity *Denki*

Cult anime Akira

BOOKS AND FILM

Japanese literature spans two millennia, but in Tokyo dates back only to the 17th-century. Since Tokyo's emergence as the centre of Japan, however, the city has produced a stream of literary innovation. Some of its foremost writers like Haruki Murakami are now global brands. Alternatively the striking, sometimes dystopian visions of a future Tokyo depicted in the popular manga comic genre have also struck a chord worldwide.

Tokyo's film industry exploded in the postwar era, with studios including Daiei, Nikkatsu, Shochiku and Toho giving rise to dramatic directors like Akira Kurosawa and animators such as Hayao Miyazaki, who thrust Japanese cinema onto the world map. Tokyo also succumbed to the predations of *Godzilla*, and provided the backdrop for a number of English-language films including the 2003 Bill Murray and Scarlett Johansson vehicle *Lost In Translation*. The latter brought renewed attention to Tokyo as an atmospheric location not only for film but for countless music and YouTube videos.

Books

Fiction

Botchan, Natsume Soseki (1906). A youthful teacher struggles to live a moral life and ultimately finds himself via a sojourn in the countryside.

Naomi, Junichiro Tanizaki (1924). Sexually frank Naomi bewitches an older man in this depiction of the loss of traditional gender roles amid encroaching Westernisation.

Snow Country, Yasunari Kawabata (1935–7). Japan's first winner of the Nobel Prize for Literature tells the story of an ill-fated affair between an urban elite and rural courtesan.

A Personal Matter, Kenzaburo Oe (1964). Peace activist and author Oe's semi-autobigraphical novel about a family dealing with their disabled son earned Japan a second Nobel Prize.

Woman in the Dunes, Kobo Abe (1962). A man becomes marooned in a village surrounded by sand and eventually embraces his fate in this Japanese modernist classic.

Sea of Fertility, Yukio Mishima (1969–71). Mishima depicted tragic love in this tetralogy – and then took his own life by sword attempting to engineer a right-wing coup in 1970.

Norwegian Wood, Haruki Murakami (1987). In recent decades Murakami has become the international face of Japanese literature on the strength of delicate yet fantastical pop fiction works like *Norwegian Wood*.

Samurai Boogie, Peter Tasker (1999). Private eye Kazuo Mori investigates the underbelly of the city. Check out the more recent Dragon Dance, also set in Tokyo.

The original Godzilla

Tokyo Stories: A Literary Stroll, translated and edited by Lawrence Rogers (2002). An anthology of stories by Japanese writers with Tokyo settings.

The Last Children of Tokyo, Yoko Tawada (2018). High satire which envisions a dystopian, surreal future Tokyo in which children are born frail and weak while the elderly seem to never die.

Non-fiction

Low City, High City: Tokyo From Edo to the Earthquake, Edward Seidensticker (1970). The entrancing history of how the city transformed from Shogun's capital to a modern metropolis.

Speed Tribes, Karl Taro Greenfeld (1994). Profiles of Tokyo's subterranean youth culture amid the go-go Bubble years.

Embracing Defeat: Japan in the Wake of World War II, John W. Dower (1999). The MIT history professor's account of Japan's rise from the ashes of WWII is a masterfully empathic retelling of the Tokyo war crimes trials and the unusual relationship between MacArthur and Emperor Hirohito.

Tokyo Vice: An American Reporter on the Police Beat in Japan, Jake Adelstein (2009). The memoir of Adelstein's years in Tokyo as the first non-Japanese reporter on the crime beat for one of Japan's largest newspapers. A film version, starring Daniel Radcliffe in the lead role, has been mooted.

Feel & Think: A New Era of Tokyo Fashion, various authors (2011). A useful introduction for anyone interested in Tokyo's vibrant and unique fashion scene.

Film

Tokyo Story (1953). Yasujiro Ozu's story about the generation gap transposes into a meditation on mortality.

Godzilla (1954). Ishiro Honda's mythic monster emerges from the sea, incensed at the testing of nuclear bombs, to wreak havoc on Tokyo.

You Only Live Twice (1967). Lewis Gilbert's Bond movie with Sean Connery, features Japanese actors and Tokyo locations, including Hotel New Otani in Akasaka and Yoyogi Stadium.

Ring (1998). Hideo Nakata's horror mystery follows a reporter and single mother who is entangled in a series of deaths related to a cursed video tape. The film spawned a host of Western remakes.

Battle Royale (2000). Kinji Fukasaku's last film stars Takeshi Kitano as a boy dealing with the death of his father who is forced to compete in a game where students must kill each other to win.

Spirited Away (2001). Hayao Miyazaki's portrait of children who enter a Japanese netherworld was the country's highest-grossing film of all time, and won a 2003 Academy Award for Best Animated Feature.

Lost In Translation (2003). Sofia Coppola dramatises the closeness that develops between two Americans who find themselves adrift in Tokyo.

Like Father, Like Son (2013). Hirokazu Koreeda's depiction of the bonding between two families whose sons are switched at birth won the director a Jury Prize at the Cannes Film Festival.

ABOUT THIS BOOK

This *Explore Guide* has been produced by the editors of Insight Guides, whose books have set the standard for visual travel guides since 1970. With top-quality photography and authoritative recommendations, these guidebooks bring you the very best routes and itineraries in the world's most exciting destinations.

BEST ROUTES

The routes in the book provide something to suit all budgets, tastes and trip lengths. As well as covering the destination's many classic attractions, the itineraries track lesser-known sights, and there are also excursions for those who want to extend their visit outside the city. The routes embrace a range of interests, so whether you are an art fan, a gourmet, a history buff or have kids to entertain, you will find an option to suit.

We recommend reading the whole of a route before setting out. This should help you to familiarise yourself with it and enable you to plan where to stop for refreshments – options are shown in the 'Food and Drink' box at the end of each tour.

For our pick of the tours by theme, consult Recommended Routes for… (see pages 6–7).

INTRODUCTION

The routes are set in context by this introductory section, giving an overview of the destination to set the scene, plus background information on food and drink, shopping and more, while a succinct history timeline highlights the key events over the centuries.

DIRECTORY

Also supporting the routes is a Directory chapter, with a clearly organised A–Z of practical information, our pick of where to stay while you are there and select restaurant listings; these eateries complement the more low-key cafés and restaurants that feature within the routes and are intended to offer a wider choice for evening dining. Also included here are some nightlife listings, plus a handy language guide and our recommendations for books and films about the destination.

ABOUT THE AUTHORS

American writer, editor and producer, Dan Grunebaum's formative Tokyo experiences date from the high-living Bubble years through the financial crisis, 2011 disaster and subsequent rebound. He never tires of the protean metropolis and has written and produced features on Japanese culture for The New York Times, CNN, Newsweek, Interview, Metropolis, NHK and NTV. Dan also produces Japanese music and performing arts showcase Saiko (saiko.co).

CONTACT THE EDITORS

We hope you find this Explore Guide useful, interesting and a pleasure to read. If you have any questions or feedback on the text, pictures or maps, please do let us know. If you have noticed any errors or outdated facts, or have suggestions for places to include on the routes, we would be delighted to hear from you. Please drop us an email at hello@insightguides.com. Thanks!

CREDITS

Explore Tokyo

Editor: Sian Marsh
Author: Dan Grunebaum
Head of DTP and Pre-Press: Rebeka Davies
Updated By: Dan Stables
Managing Editor: Carine Tracanelli
Picture Editor: Tom Smyth
Cartography: original cartography Original Cartography, updated by Carte
Photo credits: Alamy 28/29T, 36/37, 41L, 64/65, 106, 107, 116, 122, 136, 137; **Chris Stowers/Apa Publications** 4ML, 4MC, 4MR, 4MR, 4MC, 6MC, 6ML, 6BC, 8ML, 12/13, 13, 14, 15, 16, 20, 22/23, 25, 28MR, 58, 59, 61L, 62, 68/69, 70/71, 75, 94, 97, 112, 113, 124/125, 129, 130, 133, 134/135; **Corbis** 83; **Getty Images** 7M, 6TL, 8MR, 17, 35, 42/43, 51, 60, 72, 78, 79, 91, 123; **Hyatt Hotels** 104; **iStock** 4/5T, 4ML, 7T, 8ML, 10/11, 12L, 18, 28MC, 31L, 32, 32/33, 40/41, 45, 54, 57, 63L, 64, 70, 71L, 77B, 77T, 80, 86, 88, 90, 93, 95, 117, 118, 131, 132; **Jan Christopher Becke/AWL Images Ltd** 1; **JNTO** 33L, 82, 84/85, 86/87, 87L, 89, 92, 110, 111, 119; **Leonardo** 98MR, 98MC, 101, 108, 109; **Mandarin Oriental** 100; **Mary Evans Picture Library** 26/27; **Ming Tang-Evans/Apa Publications** 7MR, 8MC, 8MC, 8MR, 8/9T, 21, 28ML, 28MC, 28MR, 30, 30/31, 34, 37L, 38, 40, 44, 47, 48, 50, 55, 56, 60/61, 62/63, 65L, 66, 67, 74, 81, 98ML, 98MC, 98MR, 98ML, 105, 114, 115, 120, 121, 126; **New Otani** 103; **Nowitz Photography/Apa Publications** 18/19, 24, 28ML, 36, 39, 46, 76, 127, 128; **Okura Hotels & Resorts** 102; **Public domain** 26; **Shutterstock** 7MR, 19L, 49, 52/53, 73, 96, 98/99T
Cover credits: Susanne Kremer/4Corners Images (main) iStock (bottom)
Printed by CTPS – China

All Rights Reserved
© 2019 Apa Digital (CH) AG and
Apa Publications (UK) Ltd

Second Edition 2019

DISTRIBUTION

UK, Ireland and Europe
Apa Publications (UK) Ltd
sales@insightguides.com
United States and Canada
Ingram Publisher Services
ips@ingramcontent.com
Australia and New Zealand
Woodslane
info@woodslane.com.au
Southeast Asia
Apa Publications (Singapore) Pte
singaporeoffice@insightguides.com
Worldwide
Apa Publications (UK) Ltd
sales@insightguides.com

SPECIAL SALES, CONTENT LICENSING AND COPUBLISHING

Insight Guides can be purchased in bulk quantities at discounted prices. We can create special editions, personalised jackets and corporate imprints tailored to your needs.
sales@insightguides.com
www.insightguides.biz

INDEX

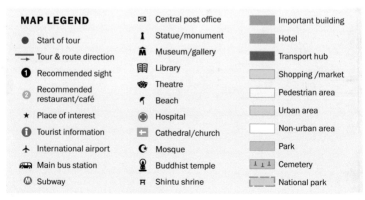

MAP LEGEND

●	Start of tour
→—	Tour & route direction
❶	Recommended sight
❷	Recommended restaurant/café
★	Place of interest
❶	Tourist information
✈	International airport
🚌	Main bus station
Ⓜ	Subway

✉	Central post office
🔱	Statue/monument
🏛	Museum/gallery
📖	Library
🎭	Theatre
⚓	Beach
⊕	Hospital
✚	Cathedral/church
☾	Mosque
🛕	Buddhist temple
卄	Shintu shrine

	Important building
	Hotel
	Transport hub
	Shopping /market
	Pedestrian area
	Urban area
	Non-urban area
	Park
┴ ┴ ┴	Cemetery
	National park